Reviews for Ryan Thorburn's *Black 14*

"Thorburn's *Black 14* is compelling on many levels. For the football fan, *Black 14* explains the impact of that 1969 autumn day on the future of Wyoming football . . . For the historian and the academic, *Black 14* takes the reader back to a fascinating time in our country's history."

—*Wyoming Lawyer*

"Thorburn covers his subject well and does justice to the most pivotal event in Wyoming football history."

—Amazon.com

"I did read the book this summer, my wife read the book this summer and we've spent a lot of time visiting about it. I think it's an important part of the history of Wyoming football, so it's something I visit with our staff about."

—Dave Christensen, Wyoming football coach to the *Casper Star-Tribune*

Lost Cowboys

The Story of Bud Daniel
and
Wyoming Baseball

Ryan Thorburn

Burning Daylight

Published by Burning Daylight, an imprint of Pearn and Associates Inc., Fort Collins, Colorado. For information about our products and services please contact happypoet@hotmail.com.

Cover design by Paperwork. Edited by Laurie Mansell Reich. Photos provided as a courtesy of the University of Wyoming Sports Information Department and Glenn Daniel.

Acknowledgments:
   The idea and inspiration for this book came from the man who built the Wyoming baseball program—Glenn "Bud" Daniel. Thanks to Bud for sharing his story, encouraging his great players to share their stories and for keeping the history and memory of UW baseball alive. I'd also like to thank Kevin McKinney for his contribution to the project. And a special thanks to the University of Wyoming Sports Information Department, especially Diane Dodson, for helping with contact information and photos.

Library of Congress Control Number: 2010929459

Thorburn, Ryan 1971
Lost Cowboys, by Ryan Thorburn. First edition.
ISBN 978-0-9841683-2-3 paper

In memory of Ray Thorburn,
one of the greatest of the Greatest Generation.

Contents

The old Wyoming slingshot logo

Foreword

I owe my love for the game of baseball to my dad. John, or "Junior" as most everyone in Cheyenne knew him, was a baseball fanatic. Sure, he was a fan of football and basketball, but it was the game of baseball and all of its nuances that fascinated him. He taught me how difficult the game was, and to respect it. He was a St. Louis Cardinals fan, primarily because their games beamed into our living room on KMOX out of St. Louis. I remember so many summer evenings sitting on our front porch listening to Harry Caray—before he was tainted by the Cubs—fill the radio with emotion as he described the ups-and-downs of our beloved Redbirds.

We couldn't really hear the games until the sun went down. That's when smaller wattage stations had to "power down," and the big 50,000-watters covered the country with clear channel signals. It would be the third or fourth inning before the static went away enough for us to hear Harry clearly. Before we heard a score, we could tell if the Cardinals were ahead or behind by the inflection of Harry's voice. My dad, mother and I made a pilgrimage to St. Louis when I was two years old to see the Cardinals and Brooklyn Dodgers play a four-game series. I don't remember a thing about it, but have the souvenirs to prove we were there.

I suspect my son, Sean, may have the same type of memories. I taught him to love and respect the game just as my dad did for me. Sean played the game much better than I ever did and produced an excellent career at the college level at Mesa State in Grand Junction,

CO. He now coaches the game on the college level. He has always made me an exceedingly proud father. One of my most memorable weekends came when my dad, Sean and I went to St. Louis and watched the Cardinals together. That was something.

When I was growing up the radio, not television, was the vehicle for my dad and me to all of baseball's brightest stars and greatest moments. My dad's heroes—especially Stan Musial—became my heroes. I know it was very disappointing to my dad when as a grade-schooler I shared my allegiance to the Cardinals with the New York Yankees. He couldn't understand it. But in my mind it was simple; they won all the time. Sure, the Cards were deep in my heart, and still are. But I always admired the pinstripes. As television matured, we looked so forward to watching the Saturday "Game of the Week," and later the World Series, so we could finally see the men we had always heard about via radio. It seemed as if the Yankees were always on the tube in those early years, and most of the time they were. But our baseball education came primarily through radio.

On rare occasions—and this was a remarkable treat—we would drive to Denver to watch the Denver Bears play in the old American Association. It wasn't the big leagues, but it was amazing nevertheless. Bears Stadium (on the site that is now Invesco Field) was the biggest building I had ever seen. While there may have been just a few thousand fans in the stadium, it was still overwhelming to me. By the way, the Bears at that time were the Triple-A farm club of the Yankees, which further strengthened my feeling for the Yanks. My dad didn't like that Yankees connection, so our trips were few and far between.

Far more often, we made the trip over the hill to Laramie to watch Wyoming play baseball. My first recollections of Cowboys baseball were in the mid-

1950s when the 'Pokes played their games at University Diamond, which was located just south of War Memorial Fieldhouse—much later that area would become Tailgate Park during football Saturdays. It was an awesome experience for me. My first Cowboys hero was Bob Jingling, who played shortstop and became an All-American. He was a heck of a hitter, and I remember how disappointed I was when my dad told me he was "signed" by the Detroit Tigers and not the Cardinals or Yankees. I could say that I had so many Cowboy heroes, but that isn't the case. Jingling was easy to follow and elevate to hero status. The only other Poke who made an impression on me in those early years was a great pitcher by the name of Pat House. To me, he was seven feet tall (I think he was actually 6' 3" or 6' 4"). We would try heading to Laramie when he was scheduled to throw.

While it wasn't as consistent as I would have liked, we did drive over to numerous Cowboy baseball games through those years, long before there was a Cowboy Field. I loved it every bit as much as I did when my dad took me to a Cowboy football or basketball game (which he did often since he "engineered" the games for Larry Birleffi). I also remember the baseball weather, something I would become so used to while watching games at Cowboy Field. We didn't have the weather channel in those days, but we would listen for the forecast to make our decision as to whether or not we'd go to Laramie. It was always a bummer if my dad decided it was probably too cold to go over. But when we did, it was a delight.

I recall coming over to the dedication of the new Cowboy Field and being very disappointed when the game was postponed due to weather. In fact, it took two or three tries before the beautiful new complex was finally officially christened. Because of schedules and my dad working on weekends, I was disappointed that I only got a chance to see a couple of games in that beautiful stadium while in junior high and high school. How could I ever imagine that I would eventually see hundreds of games in that yard before the sport was eliminated.

It was 1967 when I came to the University of Wyoming as a freshman. And it was my great fortune, due to the help of my dad and Birleffi, to receive an opportunity to work as an intern in the Sports Information Department headed up by Bill Young. I had no idea what a marvelous stroke of luck that was. I eventually would make the Athletics Department my career, thanks in large part to Bill. Not only was he one of the finest men I've ever known, Bill was a marvelous teacher and a great friend. Along with fellow interns Scott Binning and Rick Morris, and our secretary Margret Bott, we helped Bill with all areas of the athletic information business at UW. The position was far more than an internship. It was the experience of a lifetime.

Each of us was assigned a sport or two, and we all helped with football, basketball and baseball. There were no women's sports at that time. What could be better for me than being involved with baseball? I remember that first spring of baseball. Bill, Scott, Rick and I worked the games at Cowboy Field. We each had our assignments, from keeping the scorebook to the public address. It's a time I will never forget. But I would be less than honest if I didn't say there were many cold and miserable days spent at the park.

Getting to know Coach Bud Daniel was an experience. He was a pepper-pot who had to be one of the most intimidating 5' 6" individuals I ever knew. But I thought the world of him. He was a great guy with an amazing passion for the game. Nobody loved baseball like Bud, and nobody wanted to win any more than he did. He *was* Wyoming baseball. He kept it alive with his passion. And despite the weather, he always managed to recruit quality players. He was tough, but fair, from where I sat.

Birleffi once wrote a column on Daniel in the *Wyoming Eagle* after the Cowboys had won another Skyline Eastern Division title after the 1959 season. Quoting Larry:

> *(Daniel) has taken a group of college kids, who could be discouraged alone by the limited opportunity to get outdoors, and won another championship. Daniel apparently has developed a formula which produces exciting baseball and winning teams. He's recruited a nucleus from the Midwest where high school ball is played and filled in with material available in our neck of the woods. He has taken his teams into sunny Arizona while the snow still drifts at home as a conditioning jaunt. This exposes his teams to topflight college baseball, although they may take quite a cuffing around at times in the early season.*

Daniel certainly could be stubborn. The four of us would sit in the Cowboy Field press box—which could be akin to a walk-in freezer—many nights wondering why we were playing 8 p.m. games at 7,200 feet during a Wyoming spring. It would be freezing; it would often snow. But there we were, playing night baseball. Bud always told us we play night games because the new stadium—which was four years old when I started—had lights for a reason, and we were going to use them! Scott, Rick and I came up with a grand idea especially for those night games—day games as well. We cut the fingers out of wool gloves so we could hold pencils making it easier for us to keep score. Whoever was on the public address announcer could wear the regular variety.

One of my fondest memories of the old icebox was our athletics director and a Wyoming icon, Red Jacoby, leaning against the heating duct that sent warm air to the Cowboy locker room located below us. It was far and away the warmest part of that press box, and Red couldn't be pried from that spot. I'll also always have the memory of Bob Hammond, the *Laramie Boomerang* sports editor, sitting next to us. He was supposed to be an objective reporter, but make no mistake, he was rooting for the Cowboys. I can't remember exactly when, but I was assigned the public address job on a more consistent basis as our internships moved along. At least I got to wear full gloves. I ended up performing that duty until baseball was sadly eliminated in 1996. I loved being at that stadium and so looked forward to the game days. I have missed it terribly ever since. Springtime—the weather withstanding—is just not the same around the Athletics Department without baseball.

The early season, two-week spring trips to warmer climates that Birleffi talked about were invented by Daniel, and many years proved to be very tough on the Cowboys. But the 'Pokes usually would return from those trips a better baseball team. Those spring roadies were tough on those of us in Sports Information *every* year. There were no computer statistics programs in those days, and it was our job to calculate stats by hand. Bud would send us maybe six box scores at a time from his trip, and we would figure and record the accumulated stats by hand, one player at a time. It was incredibly time consuming, and not fun. But it was part of the deal, and we didn't know any better. We did it for many years until computer stat programs made the job much simpler. By the way, you haven't lived until you dictate a baseball box score by phone to a newspaper reporter. We did that after every game. Wow, that was something!

When I began school in 1967, there were names on those Cowboys box scores like Bill Stearns, Bob Peters,

Art Howe, Ev Befus, Bob Sporrer, Tom Michel, Gary Garrison, Dave Weber, Butch Simonini, Matt Sterling, Brent Foshie and Dave Brickley. That was the first team I really got to know at Wyoming. They were a bunch of tough, hard-nosed players who fit the Bud Daniel personality.

For 21 seasons, Daniel directed the fortunes of Cowboys baseball. He was the face of the sport at Wyoming. He fought for baseball every day, even though he also served as the Athletics Department's business manager. He fashioned Poke baseball into a national presence. When he stepped down he handed the reins to one of his own, Jim Jones, who played for the Cowboys during the mid-60s. In fact, Jones won a Western Athletic Conference Northern Division batting title as a player and brought an ability to teach that phase of the game as a coach. I think he was the best hitting instructor Wyoming baseball ever had. The Cowboy batting averages reflected his teaching ability, especially in the high altitude of Laramie. During the Jones era, Wyoming may not have been able to shut down an opposing lineup all the time, but it most certainly possessed the ability to outscore anyone. In his own way, Jones was as tough and competitive as his old coach. But he had a special way of transferring his knowledge of the game, especially hitting, to young student-athletes. He carried on the Poke baseball tradition in his own way and did an excellent job for Wyoming.

Along the way, Jones recruited two of the two most exciting players I ever had the good fortune of watching wear the Brown and Yellow, Bill Ewing and Greg Brock. Not only could both hit for average and power, but they were sensational clutch hitters. Both were drafted, and Brock made quite a career for himself in the big leagues. To me, the best part about them was that they were great people and tremendous ambassadors for the University of Wyoming.

Ewing's marvelous senior year of 1976 was a very special memory for me. Without question it was the greatest season by a Cowboy that I ever saw. But until I looked it up, I had forgotten just how great it was. He led the nation in home runs with 23, a record that stood for something like eight years. That was phenomenal in its own right. But he also hit .428 and drove in 66 runs. Remember, those numbers were produced during a short collegiate season. It seemed as if all of his production came in situations when the 'Pokes needed him most. By the way, he wasn't a bad centerfielder either. He could go get the baseball with the best of them. When his four-year career came to an end, he had broken 14 season and career records at Wyoming.

It was definitely difficult to see Ewing's great career come to an end. But Jones had recruited another dandy in Brock. Just two seasons after Ewing's departure, the big first baseman out of Oregon was doing a little record book rewriting himself. His junior season was memorable because he led the team in a bunch of categories including walks, runs scored and fielding percentage. While it was impossible to predict that he would produce such an outstanding major league career, Brock certainly demonstrated that it was a possibility by his play while at Wyoming. And he did it every day. He was definitely an iron horse.

I had many more favorites through the seasons. Bill Kinneberg replaced Jones and was successful in his own right. He was a heck of a guy, and he and I became very close. Jeff Huson was one of my all-time favorite Cowboys and was the best fielding shortstop I ever saw. His career in the bigs was a great study of perseverance. Wow, what a career! What I loved most about Jeff, though, is that he was always the same, great guy. I remember one year at spring training when Jeff was with the Cubs, Sean and I saw him as the team was coming into the stadium from its buses. He was so happy to see us and made us feel very special. In fact, he gave Sean one of his bats. What a thrill!

Two draft choices of the 1980s also were favorites of mine. Mike Mulvaney, who would eventually become the head baseball coach at Colorado Mines, and Kenny Lake, from St. Louis, also were special guys. Mulvaney was right up there with the greatest hitters the Cowboys ever produced. He caught and played first and was an every-day guy like Brock. I always enjoyed visiting with him years later when his Mines' teams would play against Sean at Mesa State. Lake might have been one of the most gifted players I ever saw at Wyoming. He could cover as much of centerfield as any player, and he was a great hitter. Those guys were members of Kinneberg's 1988 team, which jelled into quite a unit to put together a most memorable season.

As I write this, the memories continue to flow. I enjoyed knowing and watching so many Cowboys through the years who played the game I love. To this day, it makes me sad that baseball is no longer an intercollegiate sport at Wyoming. My son played and coached American Legion baseball at Cowboy Field. That was a thrill for me to watch him in that stadium. But I always dreamed of him playing for the Cowboys. The decision to eliminate the game from the University of Wyoming ended that dream and probably the dreams of many others. It's a shame to be sure, but it doesn't cloud those 29 seasons of memories on Willett Drive that I will always cherish.

— KEVIN McKINNEY
MAY 2010

The 1956 Wyoming baseball team

CHAPTER 1

Prideful 'Pokes Ride to Omaha

Hope springs eternal, even in Laramie, Wyoming—the crack of the bat, the feel of the leather, the sting of the wind on your face at Cowboy Field.

In 1956, the University of Wyoming (UW) baseball team had more than hope as a promising new season appeared on the dark horizon in the dead of a High Plains winter. A special group of players assembled by a legendary coach gathered determined to finish the season playing on a field of dreams in Omaha, NE.

"The team made up its mind," Glenn "Bud" Daniel, the Hall of Fame UW baseball coach, recalled 54 years later, "we were going to the College World Series (CWS)."

Some UW baseball historians will argue that in 1955 the Cowboys fielded the best team in the program's proud history. Daniel concedes that it was his most physically gifted group.

Bob Jingling had Major League talent and was surrounded by other high-quality collegiate players such as Ron Drost, Steve Knezevich, Richard Olenick and Herb Manig.

"After Wyoming, Jingling signed with the Detroit Tigers organization, which was a big deal back then for us," said Ralph Vaughan, the 'Pokes' ace during the 1955-56 seasons. "He was one fine ball player. He was the best ballplayer I was ever on the field with. He had major league written all over him. Why he quit the game I'll never know. He was one fine man and one fine ball player."

In 1954, Jingling earned All-American honors after hitting .425 and leading his club in doubles, home runs and total bases. A total of six UW players made the all-conference team after the 'Pokes won their first Skyline Conference title, finishing with a 22-11 record.

"The three-year dynasty was born," Daniel said.

In '54, Texas and Arizona had grown tired of battling one another to get out of the regional final and represent District 6 in Omaha. Longhorns coach Bibb Falk persuaded the NCAA to place the rival Wildcats into District 7 to challenge Colorado State College (now Northern Colorado) and Wyoming in a three-team playoff for the CWS.

"We had a big press conference at the (CSC) President's office in Greeley. They decided to draw the 'peas' out of a shaker," Daniel recalled. "Pete Butler, the famous CSC coach, whispered to me as we entered the room for the drawing of the bye. He said, 'I don't know who will get the bye, but I know who will not because there ain't no Arizona pea in the bottle.'"

The Bears drew the bye. Wyoming lost to Arizona. And the Wildcats then beat CSC to go to Omaha.

That same year Daniel, one of the most respected and beloved collegiate coaches in the country, was selected to serve on the USA Olympic Baseball Committee. With only two seniors on the roster, Fred Schmidt and Bill Wilson, the Cowboys were in position to put together a dynastic run on the diamond. But the stars did not align for the star-studded lineup in 1955 either. UW captured its second consecutive Skyline Conference title, but finished with a 16-10 overall record.

"As baseball goes, it was a heart break when they failed to reach the College World Series," Daniel said.

UW players once again dominated the All-Conference selections, led by Jingling (.419), Don Napierkowski (.339), Bob Sullivan (.339), and Fritz Heiss (.298). Ed

Litecky, a key utility player overlooked when it came to postseason honors, was the team's RBI and home run leader.

"We had a better team in 1955," said Vaughan, who was 6-0 on the mound that season. "But there was just something about the 1956 team. We refused to lose. Our goal was to make it to Omaha in 1956 after coming up one game short in 1955."

Joe Gordon, a Hall of Fame player with the New York Yankees, scouted the 1955 'Pokes while working in the Detroit Tigers organization.

"Gordon spent most of the spring following Jingling, our shortstop," Daniel said. "He told me, 'If you had one more pitcher you might have gone all the way to the national championship. Overall, position by position, you were the best.'"

"Close counts only in horseshoes."

Wyoming came close but was unable to catch Northern Colorado. The Bears, who made their CWS debut in 1953, beat the 'Pokes to Omaha again in 1955.

"We don't discuss that too far," Heiss said when asked if the 1955 Cowboys were the best team he played on. "My thought is that team had a lot of individual talents, and we just couldn't put it together when we needed it. But in 1956 we blended better."

Despite losing Jingling, a two-time All-American, as well as Drost, Knezevich, Olenick and Manig, the 1956 Wyoming Cowboys were determined to make history.

Jim Hoppe, a smooth fielder, had the unenviable task of filling Jingling's shoes at the start of the campaign. Daniel decided to move Hoppe, a sophomore, to second base and inserted senior Gerry Nagle at shortstop.

"Hoppe was making the plays, but he was also making too many errors," Sullivan recalled. "We got Nagle in there at shortstop and I don't think he made an error all season. And he was a big guy. He couldn't cover the ground like Jingling or Hoppe, but he did not make an error."

Napierkowski, a senior All-American, and Sullivan returned in the outfield. The 'Pokes also added Pete Kutches, a senior outfielder borrowed from Phil Dickens' football team. Two more seniors, Heiss (first base) and Frank Goodie (third base) manned the corners. Senior pitchers Bill Meeboer, Mort Drury and Bob Villasenor added a little depth to the staff behind the ace Vaughan. Jack Hall, another senior football player, filled in on the mound and as a utility player in the field. Daniel had the luxury of two solid catchers in Robert Fisher and Dave Gossin. Completing the squad were utility players Vic McElroy and Bud Nelson. Team trainer Courtney Skinner was another important member of the program.

"We all got along well. There were no cliques. We were just a closer group as a whole than any other year," Sullivan said. "We always looked forward to those trips to Arizona and New Mexico in the spring. Regardless of wins and losses, we were getting our spring training in and the team developed by virtue of that. We found out we had a bunch of good guys and it was a good ball club."

The scoreboard indicated otherwise early in the season as the Cowboys limped back to Laramie with a 5-7 record.

"The spring trip was a disappointment. We came home with a real challenge," Daniel said. "But we caught fire and won our last six conference games."

Wyoming captured its third consecutive Skyline Conference championship after finishing league play with an 11-3 record. The 'Pokes would face Utah in a three-game playoff series in Salt Lake City with a trip to the District 7 Regional on the line. In Game 1, Hoppe singled in the ninth and eventually scored on a slow roller by Napierkowski in a 6-4 UW win. In Game 2,

Utah answered with a 9-2 victory. And in the decisive Game 3, Vaughan pitched a three-hitter to lead Wyoming to a clinching 4-1 victory.

"The game at Utah to win the Conference championship . . . that was really big," Vaughan said.

Next up: Those pesky Bears. Wyoming was an 8-5 winner in Game 1 in Greeley. The series moved to Laramie for the final two games. Northern Colorado took Game 2 by a score of 8-3 to set up one final showdown between the regional rivals with a trip to the 1956 CWS on the line.

"It was a tough series that we had. They were actually the best baseball program in the state of Colorado year in and year out," Sullivan said. "I can't remember what the score was in the final game, but there were a lot of runs scored and it was a tight one. I remember there were a lot of fly balls and line drives and we caught a lot of them."

The Cowboys seized an early 6-1 lead, but the Bears battled back and led 7-6 entering the seventh inning.

"I remember it was a wild, high-scoring ballgame," said Vaughan, an old-school knuckleball pitcher who found a way to win in the thin air of Wyoming. "We would get way ahead, and then they would get way ahead."

UW scored three runs in the seventh and held on for the thrilling 9-7 victory. Every player on the Cowboys hit safely in a 14-hit attack, led by Hoppe (3-for-5). Vaughan was credited with the win, but not before Sullivan dashed the Bears' final comeback bid with a spectacular over-the-shoulder catch on a dead run in the top of the ninth with two runners in motion, clinching the elusive berth in the CWS.

"When we finally won it was like a dream," Vaughan said. "We had done it. . . . I'm sure we celebrated. I can't remember what we did, nothing too fancy. It was a sense of pride. We pulled together as a team and pulled it out."

Daniel immediately went to the UW Fieldhouse to begin planning for the trip to Omaha.

"I told the players to go celebrate, following my rules for mature actions, of course," Daniel said.

Heiss, Nagle, Napierkowski, Sullivan and Vaughan were all selected to the NCAA All-District 7 team.

Wyoming arrived in Omaha for the 1956 CWS with 16 players, while most of the other teams had 25-man rosters.

"In 1956 the CWS was a much more exclusive championship than it is today," Daniel noted.

The current CWS model also welcomes eight teams to Omaha in a double-elimination bracket, but only after they have played their way through a 64-team NCAA tournament. In 1956, Wyoming joined Arizona, Bradley, Minnesota, Mississippi, New Hampshire, New York and Washington State at Rosenblatt Stadium. The Cowboys opened up with a 4-0 loss to Minnesota, the Big Ten champions who went on to win the national title.

"That was big-time stuff," Vaughan said. "I was afraid we would be nervous, but we got good press in Omaha, and we felt relaxed. I knew nothing about Minnesota. They were just another team to me. We played them close, and we just couldn't get any hits. Their left-hander threw a one-hitter. It was the only game we were ever shutout in my two years. We just couldn't get any runs across. You hold somebody to four runs, you feel like you ought to beat them."

Daniel's squad bounced back nicely with an 8-3 thrashing of New York University (NYU).

"Bob (Villasenor) pitched the best game he had pitched against New York University," Vaughan said. "And we beat them pretty bad."

Bradley ended UW's dream season with a 12-8 victory over the Cowboys, who settled for a final national ranking of No. 6.

"We ran out of pitching," Vaughan said. "I came in as a reliever against Bradley, and they hit me hard. We just ran out of gas. We didn't have the depth. Only 10 of our 16 players had really played. But we were proud of how far we did make it."

Over the next 40 years, Wyoming fielded some other very good teams and produced some great players. But the '56 Cowboys were the only group that ever made it to the CWS.

"I think we just tried too hard and we had a lot of things go wrong in those losses," Heiss said. "But we walked out of there with our heads held high knowing we did something that no one else will do."

In May 2010, as they do every two years, members of Daniel's teams gathered together for a reunion to celebrate the unbreakable bond that comes from playing baseball at UW.

"I tell my grandkids I pitched in the CWS," Vaughan said. "When you look back at all the teams in the country that were trying to get there, to think you were one of the teams that actually made it is something I'm very proud of. We represented ourselves well."

*Glenn "Bud" Daniel, Wyoming Cowboys
freshman catcher, 1941*

CHAPTER 2

Leader of Men (and Cowboys)

Glenn Robert "Bud" Daniel was born in Belleville, Kansas in 1923, after his grandfather and father rode in the Oklahoma Land Rush to stake out their piece of the American dream.

The family moved frequently as his dad's job with the railroad dictated. Bud attended schools in four different states. It was in Salina, KS, where his baseball skills blossomed. His American Legion team won the state championship, and he was an all-state catcher at the age of 13. As a kid, Bud fell in love with the St. Louis Cardinals, listening to the descriptions of the "Gas House Gang" on the radio.

The Daniel family moved to Lincoln, NE, when Bud was in high school and then relocated again to Casper before his senior year in 1941. Baseball wasn't a sanctioned high school sport in Wyoming. It still isn't. That didn't stop Bud from forming a team at Natrona County High School. A childhood friend of his from Kansas, who had moved to Cheyenne, also started a team at Cheyenne East High School, and the two schools would meet that year in the only high school baseball game in Wyoming history.

"Casper was a booming oil town at that time. I really enjoyed it," Daniel said. "Natrona is a good high school and it was a fun place to play. I played basketball."

In the fall of 1941, Daniel arrived in Laramie as a freshman at the University of Wyoming. His skills on the hardwood came in handy considering legendary basketball coach Ev Shelton also was coaching baseball at UW.

Daniel worked at the soda fountain in the Student Union along with Ditch Bailey. They would often play friendly games of two-on-two against basketball stars Kenny Sailors—the inventor of the jump shot—and Jimmy Weir.

"My claim to fame in basketball is one time I faked Kenny out of position and hit a jump shot," Daniel said. "He was a big name."

Sailors would lead Wyoming to an NCAA championship in 1943. But not before the innocent glory days on campus were interrupted by a call to duty.

Nearly 70 years later, Daniel still remembers the moment on Dec. 7, 1941, when news arrived in Laramie that the Japanese had attacked Pearl Harbor, as if it happened yesterday.

"It was a Sunday morning and I was at the Student Union working in the fountain room," Daniel said. "The news came over the radio and guys and gals were crying and hugging and had no idea what it really meant. It was bedlam."

Daniel enlisted in the U.S. Navy and was part of the V-5 Aviation Program. Fourteen months later he graduated from the Corpus Christi Naval Aviation Center and was commissioned a 2nd Lieutenant in the U.S. Marine Corps. After being stationed at El Toro, CA, where Daniel flew the F4U Corsair, it was on to the Pacific Theatre. Daniel departed from San Diego aboard the CVE-76 "Jeep" aircraft carrier.

Daniel's assignment was dangerous, but flattering, for a 19-year-old kid from Wyoming. He was the wingman for legendary Marine ace Major Robert "Cowboy" Stout, a UW graduate from Fort Laramie, during the Battle of Peleliu, an island located about 500 miles east of the Philippines.

Lt. Bud Daniel and Major Robert "Cowboy" Stout, USMC. Daniel was "Cowboy's" Wingman during the Battle of Peleliu, in WWII. Both Stout and his younger brother Jack, from Ft. Laramie, Wyoming, were killed flying Corsairs in WWII.

"Every day you got up in the airplane you never thought about it," Daniel said of the bloody war of attrition against the Imperial Japanese Army. "But you were in the combat zone and anything could happen."

Stout and his younger brother, Jack, who Daniel had worked with at the Student Union back in Laramie, were both combat casualties.

"When (Robert) Stout got killed it was a terrible event. I was there when he got a wing blown off, and I got hit too," Daniel said. "I had a couple scary events."

Daniel survived another close call after flying into the eye of a major storm and then flying back just over the ocean waves in the dark. He did his best to stay in touch with his parents by writing letters; his mom mailed Spam for him to eat throughout his 18 months of service overseas.

Upon returning stateside in May 1945, Daniel flew for the Navy Ferry Squadron until the war ended. His combat decorations included the Distinguished Flying Cross, the Air Medal with two Gold Stars, the Purple Heart and the Navy Unit Citation.

Daniel, who served in the USMC Reserve from 1946-56 and then transferred to the Wyoming National Guard, returned to UW in January of 1946.

As a UW player, Daniel had a three-year batting average of .482. On two occasions during the 1948 season he went 6-for-6 at the plate and had eight consecutive hits over a two-game span. On May 5, 1948, Daniel's 25th birthday, he hit for the cycle.

After graduation, Daniel became a teacher and basketball coach at Cody High School. One of his players was a lanky kid by the name of Alan Simpson, the future U.S. Senator from Wyoming.

"Bud was the head coach and I was the team captain. We had a good season and won the district championship, but then we got cocky," Simpson recalled. "We thought we were going to beat Cheyenne and Casper at state, and we didn't beat Lusk. I was a mess. I guess we had read our press clippings. But that was the players' fault, Bud was a good coach."

In July 1950, Glenn "Red" Jacoby, UW's visionary athletic director, hired Daniel with the title of athletic business manager/head baseball coach.

The Cowboys were 7-9 during the 1951 season that spring. Daniel, a fiery competitor, quickly realized that UW baseball needed to start thinking—and recruiting—outside the box.

"My first season was a learning season of the fact that we would have to expand our program both with scholarships, recruiting and a larger game schedule," Daniel said.

Since there was not sanctioned high school baseball in Wyoming, and a limited American Legion baseball presence, Daniel made a New Year's resolution on January 1, 1951: "To check the spring sports pages of all Chicago papers on file in Wyoming's library each week to assemble a prospect list of high school baseball players in the greater Chicago area."

Jacoby—who had overseen nationally competitive basketball and football programs—granted the young coach permission to formulate a program of tuition, board and room, books and fees for prospective recruits for the baseball program. The travel schedule and budget were also expanded, and an athletic dorm program was established.

"Jacoby was hard-nosed, very competent and under-standing of his staff's needs in order to work to be a success," Daniel said. "In my many years that I worked for him he never turned me down when I submitted a well-organized and sensible request. You had to be well aware of his requirements in order to succeed."

Daniel drove from Laramie to Chicago with football coach Bowden Wyatt, who was one of the coaches in the College-Pro All-Star Game at Soldier Field. The plan proved to be a brilliant one considering the all-city high school baseball semifinals were also taking place at the University of Chicago.

The Bowen High School team immediately caught Daniel's attention. He asked the coach, Harry Pritican, if he could meet with the talented prep players after their game to tell them about the new baseball opportunities being offered at Wyoming. Soon after speaking to the wide-eyed kids in the outfield, Daniel was doing a recruiting dance with the parents.

"My recruiting policy was to establish their desire for a college education first and explain to the parents that baseball at the University of Wyoming could be the means to an end of their attaining a college degree," Daniel said. "I explained in detail what I would expect from them on and off of the baseball diamond, and what the scholarship would provide—board and room, tuition, books and fees for four years."

Seven of Bowen's nine starters arrived at the train station in Laramie in the fall of 1952. Many of them contributed to the program's run of three consecutive Skyline Conference titles and the 1956 appearance in the CWS. All of them would leave with a life-changing degree from UW.

"There was some culture shock getting off the train in Laramie the first time," said Herb Manig, one of the great UW players recruited out of Chicago by Daniel. "After Bud met me and got me set up, I walked down-town on University Avenue. While I was gazing up at the mountains I heard commotion down to the south of me and there were two guys dragging a third guy out of one of the saloons and beating up on him. "I thought, 'welcome to the wild west.'"

The 1952 and 1953 seasons were as inconsistent as the Cowboys' 12-11 overall record during that two-year span suggests. Daniel remained focused on the long-term vision for the program, knowing that the Chicago freshmen were making the difficult transition from high school to college while learning through mistakes.

"I felt confident that they would be outstanding the next season," Daniel said.

After the glory days of 1954-56, Wyoming baseball remained competitive with CWS holdovers Jim Hoppe, Dave Gossin and Mort Drury while reloading with future stars such as John Phillips, Bill Lutz, Norm Sagara, Tommy Thomas, Mike Cooke and Cody's Bill Cheney.

In the fall of 1958, tragedy struck the program as two players from Billings, MT, Tommy Thomas and Dennis Seiler, were asphyxiated in their off campus apartment as a result of a faulty heater. After leaving UW to begin serving in the Air Force, Napierkowski, a beloved All-American player for the 'Pokes, also tragically was killed in a car accident while on active duty.

"Our club mourned their loss," Daniel said. "It was devastating to our fall practice."

In 1958, Wyoming's greatest baseball fan—Pat Murray, a retired U.S. Army Artillery Colonel and member of the 1912 U.S. Olympic pole-vaulting team—started leading the Cowboy caravan from Laramie to California and Arizona for the team's annual spring trip, driving his signature Cadillac.

"Colonel Murray left his wife every spring with the statement, 'I'm going to a ballgame, see you later,'" Daniel said. "He was the team scorekeeper. He furnished his Cadillac for away games and had a new one every two years. He kept players fascinated with his 'Klondike Stories.'

"When the games were snowed out, his card tricks mesmerized the gang. In his eighties he still taught players to lead off first base with a hook slide. He needed a surgical hernia repair after one too many attempts."

Coach Daniel and Col. Murray

Spring training 1955, Tempe, Arizona. From left (front)
Napierkowski, Sullivan, Drost, Manig; (back) Goodie, Litecky

Poolside, from left
Litecky, Bromley,
Nagle, Drost, and
Napierkowski

Col. Murray remained an indelible part of the Cowboys baseball program until his death in 1971.

"His stories and antics on and off the field were memories to file forever," Daniel said. "He was a fine golfer and made certain that I would see that his burial plot was on the corner of the fifth hole at Warren Air Force Base Golf Course in Cheyenne.

"On his deathbed, (my wife) Connie had kissed him goodbye, and he was still able to pinch her on the bottom as we left him."

Oliver Knight, Joe Cook, Dave Hurwitz and John Deti were also among the Wyoming baseball supporters who volunteered to drive their automobiles on the team's annual spring trips to the Southwestern states.

"These men enjoyed being with the young athletes for the many hours required for traveling and playing games," Daniel said. "Only John Deti ever found it difficult. In the middle of one of the trips he asked if he could return to Laramie. When I ask him why? His answer was: 'In my entire married life I have never spent a full 24 hours away from her.'

"Homesick he was, but John gutted it out."

Wyoming, despite playing most of its games on the road, was a respectable 50-57 from 1957-60.

In 1961, led by ace and future Major League pitcher Pat House, the Cowboys finished 17-13 overall and won the program's fourth Skyline Conference title.

In 1962, the year of the Cuban Missile Crisis, Daniel was called back to active duty with the Wyoming National Guard. Bob Jingling, the two-time All-American shortstop for UW during the great run in the mid-50s, filled in as head coach that season. The Cowboys finished 11-15 in the final season of the Skyline Conference before joining the Western Athletic Conference (WAC).

During his recall, Daniel was selected to represent the American Baseball Coaches Association (ABCA) and the U.S. Olympic Committee in Japan. The meetings were with the Secretary General of the Olympic Organizing Committee, with the goal of including baseball as a demonstration sport in the 1964 Tokyo Games.

"Upon my return from Japan, the military powers at Ft. Lewis, WA realized that Captain Daniel in civilian life was the baseball coach at the University of Wyoming," Daniel said. "With the emergency activation of the famous Army 'Big Red One Division' from Wisconsin, they suddenly had 25 big league and Triple-A players on active duty."

Daniel would be the commissioned officer assigned to coach the group, which had special service duty to provide recreation entertainment for the troops. The team included Tony Kubek (New York Yankees), George Thomas (Boston Red Sox), Deron Johnson (Oakland Athletics) and Gary Cowan (future UW baseball assistant coach). Daniel guided the stacked squad to a 34-1 record.

"I was extremely pleased to have this fortunate and most interesting assignment," Daniel said.

In 1963, Daniel returned to Laramie to coach as UW entered a new conference, the WAC, and began playing in a beautiful new ballpark, Cowboy Field.

The 1954 Wyoming baseball team, which won the first of the Cowboys' three consecutive Skyline Conference championships.

Back row (from left): Bud Daniel (coach), Fritz Heiss, Steve Knezevich, Don Napierkowski, Ron Drost, Ed Litecky, Dick Olejnik. Middle row: Bob Jingling, Fred Schmidt, Bill Wilson, Bob Villasenor, Thornton Bromley, Nick Popravak. Front: Bob Sullivan, Courtney Skinner (trainer) and Jerry Nagle.

CHAPTER 3

"Wyoming baseball has been good to me"

Thornton Bromley, pitcher 1951–55

I had no intention of going to college or playing baseball after high school, but when Bud Daniel came to my house in July 1951, it changed my entire life. Graduating from Wyoming allowed me the opportunity to pursue a job teaching and coaching, as well as a career in golf management and construction.

I will be forever in debt to Coach Daniel for giving me the opportunity for a better life for myself and my family. UW will always hold a special place in my heart.

The incident that I remember best on the field involved pitcher Mort Drury. We were sitting by the fence down in left field talking about the game and pitching, when he noticed that I had a big chew in my mouth. He asked me what I was chewing, and I answered tobacco. It was really some raisins, but I always had a plug of tobacco in my pocket. I would on occasion chew that.

I asked Mort if he would like to try a chew, and he said sure. I gave him some tobacco and about five minutes later he started running to the Fieldhouse. I forgot to tell him not to swallow the juice, but to be sure to spit it out. He refrained from talking to me for about two weeks.

(Author's note: Bromley graduated from UW in 1955 with a Bachelor's Degree in Education. He is a retired educator, coach and business executive.)

Norm Sagara, infielder 1958-59

Fred Answine, from Jeannette, PA, shared this story with me at one our Lander gatherings:

Fred was a terrific left-handed hitter, but he had two right hands when it came to playing defense. He would have been the epitome of the "Designated Hitter (DH)," had the DH been allowable back in 1959. Bud Daniel needed Fred's presence in the lineup because of his bat, so one game he deployed him in leftfield with specific instructions that he was to stand on the foul line and any ball hit in the field of play he was to let me or Pat Thorpe take care of. His area of responsibility was from the foul line to the foul area fence only. However, there was no disputing his ability with the bat.

In the 1959 season, Thorpe, a sophomore outfielder from Denver's Regis High School, was having a so-so season, hitting below his potential. Coach was perceptive enough to pick up some holes in his swing and suggested changes in his approach. We were halfway through the season, and Pat was hitting .277 through 13 games. After making the adjustments Daniel had suggested, Pat went on to capture the team batting championship and finished that season with a .337 average.

There were two Bills on our ball club, both pitchers: known as Bill No. 1 and Bill No. 2. It seems Daniel was being interviewed by a reporter from the *Laramie Boomerang* about a very important upcoming game when he was asked about his choice for the starting pitcher for the Cowboys. Coach responded by saying,

"I'm still going with Bill No. 1 because he is like money in the bank."

Bill No. 2 was so upset with that quote that he never forgot about it. To this day, the saying "Money in the Bank" gets him hot under the collar and riled up.

(*Author's note:* Sagara, who transferred to UW from a junior college, graduated in 1960 with a Bachelor's Degree in Education and became a teacher.)

Paul Hook, outfield 1957

After competing in baseball in the United States Army in France in 1953 and 1954, where I was selected as "France's finest," I was offered a baseball scholarship to the University of Wyoming.

I was only able to participate at UW one year (1957) due to a torn quadricep muscle in my right leg. I returned to Indiana, had the leg operated on and finished my degree at Indiana State University.

But it was a great year playing for the Cowboys. I finished the season with a .307 batting average. I'm grateful to coach Bud Daniel for advising me to switch to the correct swing techniques that really improved my hitting.

On the southern trip, I was the only player to get a hit off Arizona's Don Lee, who later pitched in Major League Baseball. He was able to finish a one-hit game against the Cowboys. I also remember hitting a home run against Air Force.

After teaching for 32 years I retired. I am proud to have had the opportunity to play one season and letter in baseball at UW. I wish my injury had not prevented me from contributing more to the program.

Jim MacDonnell, pitcher 1966-69

I reviewed my college record from a scrapbook kept then by my wife-to-be, Kathy, who I'm still married to. I was average in physical skills. The reason Bill Kimball—a scout for the Chicago White Sox—recommended me to be drafted was because he thought I was intelligent and could get stronger.

Triple-A was the maximum level for my skill set. I only harbor great thoughts and memories from the minor leagues an am not upset about never getting the call up to the big leagues. I always thought I was darn fortunate to receive a scholarship to play college baseball. I was the oldest of nine children, and I felt responsible to lower the family's overhead for my education. I had several scholarship offers but went to Wyoming because it was 135 miles from my younger eight siblings. I wanted to be relatively close and help them when I could. When my dad and I made a recruiting visit to UW we had cheeseburgers and chili at a bowling alley near the campus with Bud Daniel. The coach offered me a full ride, less a payment of $150 per semester.

I was really excited, and it got even better when Bob Wilson, a basketball player from Denver, ended up being my roommate. Other Denver athletes on campus included Tom Asbury, Carl Ashley and the Wilson brothers in basketball; Corbin, Stearns, Adair, Bozich, Sterling and myself in baseball. As freshmen we were ineligible, so I remember listening to the UW-Arizona conference playoff game in Laramie on the radio while I studied in my dorm room for a final exam. That was the last year freshmen were ineligible. I don't think the incoming crop of freshmen, primarily from Billings, MT, realized how lucky they were.

Playing in Hawaii was quite memorable. As I recall, we drove to California for the Riverside Tournament before flying to Hawaii. That was my first trip on an airplane. In my business travels over the last 24 years I have racked up easily 1.5 million miles in the air.

I think our stay at the Marine Corps Recruit Depot in San Diego my junior year holds the most memories for me. I was having a very good season with three or four consecutive wins. It was always amazing to me that the first time we played outdoors was the first game of our season. I thought we did awfully well in spite of preparing indoors at the old Armory. Martin Luther King, Jr. was killed in Tennessee during our stay. San Diego also experienced a real strong earthquake and our beds danced on the concrete floors and the telephone poles swayed back and forth.

Matt Sterling and David Brickley, who are now deceased, were out drinking late one night and tried to get back on the base, but the Shore Patrol would not let them in. Eventually, they realized they were at the Navy base, not the Marine base.

We normally played a game in the afternoon in San Diego, and then we would have to wait for the Marine Corps bus to pick us up to take us back to the depot. The games would often finish as the sun was setting and the cold fog rolled in. Daniel always got picked up in a red sports car with his wife Connie at the wheel. Once while we were waiting for our bus, Bob Sporrer lost his patience, reached into the equipment bag and hit all the balls into the Pacific Ocean.

(*Author's note:* MacDonnell earned a Bachelor's Degree from UW in Business in 1969. He played three seasons for the Chicago White Sox Triple-A team and is currently a business manager in Denver.)

Ron Drost, catcher 1952-55

In March of 1952 there was snow on the ground in Laramie, but I was about to embark on my first trip to the southwest with the Wyoming baseball team where we would engage Arizona, New Mexico, Denver and a few military teams. I was the varsity catcher from 1952-55. As I recall, the first season was tough since most of the team was made up of freshmen, along with seniors Gus Angelos and Tom Bournellis.

After that first year, we improved and won back-to-back Skyline titles in '54 and '55. I graduated in '56 with a degree in Physical Education. I wanted to get into coaching, but saw the Marine OSO in the Student Union and signed up. My blood pressure was a problem getting past the physical. Bud Daniel and I made a few trips to Denver to finally pass the blood pressure hurdle. After graduation, I went to Worland and played for Nick Johnson that summer while working for the Sterns-Rogers and Holly Sugar Company.

In January, I reported to Quantico for the OCC class. I was commissioned a 2nd Lieutenant on 1 April 1957 and reported to The Basic School at Camp Upshur. I was then ordered to the 2nd Mar Div in December 1957, where I spent two years with the 8th Marines & 2nd AntiTank Battalion. In June 1959, I was ordered to HQMC to be briefed on duty aboard a new concept ship, LPH4. I spent two years of sea duty, out of Norfolk, VA, then on to Little Creek, VA for duty with LFTU. I was one of the first to fire the ARI5, which would become the M-16 rifle.

After that I was ordered to the 1st Marine Brigade, in Kaneohe, Hawaii. My unit (3rd Battalion, 4th Marines) was ordered to Vietnam six months later. We landed in the city of Hue, moved south and remained there until December 24, 1965. I returned to Okinawa for rehab and then went back to Vietnam in March of 1966. I left in April, with orders to Denver as Officer In Charge of the recruiting station. I was ordered to the 3rd Marine Division, which was about to leave for Okinawa in six months, but asked for reassignment and was sent to Saigon with the Military Advisory Command. Then it was on to the district headquarters in New Orleans. Finally, I was transferred to Marine Corps Base, Camp Pendleton, CA, where I retired a Major in 1977.

I received my MBA in 1977 from National University in San Diego and started a custom furniture business with my wife that continued until 2002.

The education baseball provided me was a direct result of Daniel's confidence in me. I am eternally grateful to Coach for the opportunity I had to play ball at UW. It was, and will always be, the best time of my life.

Roger McKenzie, pitcher 1969-72

I was just sitting down with my mom to sign a letter of intent to play football at Illinois State University when a call came from Tubby Simonini asking if I would be interested in playing baseball at Wyoming. I said yes. Bud Daniel called, and I flew out to visit the campus in June. The weather was fantastic—the sky was blue, the temperature was in the 80s. Being that I had never been west, I figured that was what the weather was like all the time, and we would be playing ball all year. The first week of school, reality set in. Much to my surprise it snowed six inches. It was then that I realized what an altitude of 7,200 feet meant.

My first roommate was Vince Tolpo. I remember his art easel and his cello in our little room. We were quite the odd couple. He wanted to practice that cello in the room, so I got another roommate. Vince eventually was banned from practicing in the dorm and sent to the music hall.

I also remember coach having to ground me, at least twice. The first time three other pitchers and I did not make it back in time for curfew. Coach wisely confined us to our rooms for a few days, except for eating and playing baseball. Not learning my lesson, the next year I was caught in the wrong room after hours, and this time I was not allowed to play. We were on the spring trip, and I was sent back to stay with my dad in Arizona. I learned that there was safety in numbers.

One funny incident I remember was Conrad Bucheleon losing his toothbrush from his pocket while running to first base. Why he had his toothbrush with him while playing was a mystery.

I attended a UW baseball reunion a few years ago, and it was great. It allowed me to rekindle some old friendships and share old memories. In the years after that reunion, I reconnected with Rick O'Daniels and his wife while visiting family in Arizona. We shared many memories of our days at Wyoming. I'm glad we had those opportunities before he passed away.

Jack Herrod, pitcher 1957-61

My Wyoming experience began early in 1957 after graduating from a small high school in northern California, hitching a ride to Laramie that summer and pursuing my goal of earning a degree in Pharmacy.

I also wanted to play college baseball and was encouraged to walk on. Freshmen were not eligible to participate, so several of us worked out with the varsity and played briefly in some non-Conference games. At that time, Bud Daniel relied primarily on junior college transfers. I was fortunate and excited to be a part of the 1959 team and was given a full scholarship for the season. I had really blown it after the fall of 1958 when I was ineligible to participate in NCAA sports. This really aggravated Daniel, and justifiably so, as he had put faith and confidence in me. I spent the spring semester working out with the team and getting my academics in order.

The next two years I studied hard and enjoyed the fun of some successful baseball seasons. At that time I realized the only reason I continued my education was because I wanted to play on the baseball team. It gave me the opportunity to develop many lifetime friendships.

By my fifth year of college I matured and realized baseball would not be a vital part of my future and that pharmacy would be my career. I dropped out of baseball and wrapped up my degree. I have achieved a successful career and have a wonderful family and a wealth of great friendships. This all happened thanks to Daniel and the UW baseball program. Every day I feel blessed for the ongoing friendships I have because of this experience.

Howard Maley, infield 1960-62

My Wyoming Cowboy baseball memories begin in 1959. On graduation day in Sidney, NE, population 7,000, I was fretting about the speech I would be delivering as the Salutatorian of my graduating class of 78. But more than that I was worried about how I would be able to afford college. After the speeches were finished and the awards were being distributed, the local radio station awarded me the $200 scholarship for basketball. I was first-team in our four-town conference, so probably deserving. I was surprised when I also was named the recipient for football. Was it for playing an entire game with a broken foot I injured on the kickoff and not realizing it until I removed my shoe after the game? Whatever the reason, I had an additional $650 to go with the money I saved working summers and weekends.

There is no high school baseball program in Sidney, so, at age 17, I became the shortstop on the town team. There is not a lot to do in southwest Nebraska so there is considerable interest in baseball. The quality of play is surprisingly good, and games are well attended. Lou Thorpe, one of the prominent lawyers in town (perhaps the only one), had played college football at Wyoming. He set up a meeting with Bud Daniel in Laramie. Coach offered me a chance to compete for a spot on the team as a walk-on with the possibility of a partial scholarship if I was successful. I was very grateful to Mr. Thorpe for arranging the meeting and, after hitting all the popular watering holes in Laramie, I am quite sure he was grateful to me as well for being the designated driver.

Playing baseball in Laramie can be very challenging, beginning with the first spring practices in January in the War Memorial Fieldhouse, which was booked solid as the home of Cowboy basketball, wrestling, track, state high school basketball tournaments and off-season workouts for the football, tennis and golf programs. It is a cavernous building capable of seating the entire population of Sidney with ease, I am sure. There was an oval cinder track that surrounded the basketball court. This is where Daniel separated the men from the boys. He had us form a single line and we took turns fielding, or trying to field, his hot ground balls that jumped off that wretched, but magical, fungo bat of his.

When basketball season ended, the court was dismantled, and we had a semblance of infield and outfield for practice, as well as hitting and pitching practice in the cages. In March, the team departed for Arizona *sans* freshmen, who were not eligible for varsity sports back in the day. Upon the team's return we began outdoor practices, weather permitting. The baseball field was an adaptation of the football practice field, but to me it was the most amazing field I have ever played on. Imagine playing baseball with a grass infield. I was ecstatic at the end of the season when Daniel informed me that I had earned a baseball scholarship that paid my tuition for the 1960-61 school year.

The 1961 season began with the trip to Arizona, which was an eye-opener for someone who had only been to Pratt, KS, Denver and Laramie. It was almost inconceivable to me that a state that is not that far from Wyoming could have such beautiful, warm and sunny weather in March, with the heavy scent of oranges in full bloom. The Arizona teams that we faced were another story. They were in mid-season form having played 20 games. Looking back on it, I am amazed at how competitive the Cowboys could make most games. When given opportunities to play other cold-weather schools we were routinely winning games against Michigan, Wisconsin and other Big Ten teams.

One of my fond memories occurred during a scheduled meeting with Arizona State. It had been raining, and the game was about to be postponed. Daniel would hear nothing of it and became a one-person grounds crew. With the aid of gasoline and matches, he soon had the field, if not perfect, at least playable. We finished the season by successfully defending first place in the Eastern Division of the Skyline Conference. For some unknown reason a playoff with the Western Division winner was not scheduled. Daniel scheduled a road trip to play various town teams in Wyoming for the players who would be returning the following year. During the latter innings of one of these games, I was astonished to realize that Daniel had been the home plate umpire the entire game.

I was informed that I would be the starting second baseman for the ensuing year. With this knowledge I proudly wore my brown letter jacket with the bright yellow 'W' wherever I went.

We opened the 1962 season against formidable Arizona State. My nightmare was about to begin, some of which remains vivid even today. Early in the game I mishandled a hard-hit ground ball. The ball dribbled away from me and, in my haste to get the runner at first, I made an overthrow for a double error. The very next batter hit a pop-up to me at second. I was introduced to the "high sky" in Arizona and, to my horror, suddenly I had to dive backward but the ball again ticks off the fingers of my glove for the third error of the inning. Pat House was on the mound (he would later pitch two years in the big leagues), and he pitched very well, but we were ultimately defeated 6-4, almost entirely by the unearned runs that scored as a result of my miscues.

Things turned out better during a tight game against the Air Force Academy when I came to the plate with the bases loaded and hit a ball that got over the center fielder's head. It rolled a long way on the football practice field. Had I been a faster, it would have been the first and only home run of my college career. My triple drove in the wining runs. My only regret is not keeping the *Laramie Boomerang* clip documenting my shining moment.

It became clear to me that the Fred Brigham, the freshman shortstop from the pervious year with great hands and a strong arm, would be replacing Dick Hawthorne. That meant I would be competing with Hawthorne for the second base job. I also would be graduating with a major in Accounting in the spring and getting married to Sylvia Field of Laramie on the first of June. I really needed to schedule interviews and find a job. So I acknowledged, somewhat reluctantly, that my Cowboy baseball career had come to an end, but I would not trade one day of those four wonderful years for anything.

Gordy Westhoff, third base 1963-66

This story involves a not-so pleasant event, but it really was funny then and even funnier now. We had a blonde, right-handed pitcher from California named Ken Hemming. On our southern trip to Tempe, AZ, he was pitching a morning game and took a line drive right in the spot where no man should be hit. This does not sound funny, but what makes it so is the fact that he swore he would never wear a cup because they were so uncomfortable. When he got hit square, he went down like he was shot with an AK-47. He had to come out of the game and, by the end of the day, his "jewels" were a deep purple and the size of grapefruit.

That night we went to the local pizza shop down the street from our motel and pretty much the entire team helped him drown his pain because he was really miserable. He was a focused Business major and not the partier as many of us were—in fact I had never seen him drink before that night. We got him feeling pretty good, but he literally could not walk due to the pain, and we had to carry him back to the motel. We were all afraid one of Bud Daniel's graduate assistants would see us.

Johnny Omohundro was with us and, when we got Ken home, the great Cowboy trainer made him go to sleep with a bag of ice. Hemming missed about 3-4 weeks and, when he did finally come back, he did wear a cup. He was a really good student, a very serious kid who had to take a lot of ribbing from the team. He had a girlfriend in California and was planning on marrying her after he graduated, but we had him convinced that he would probably not be able to consummate the marriage. The morning after Hemming's injury, the entire pitching staff made a mad dash to the local sporting goods store to purchase metal athletic support cups.

(*Author's note:* Westhoff captained the Cowboys in 1966; the team won the WAC's Northern Division that season. He graduated from UW with a Bachelor's Degree in Education [1967] and a Master's Degree in Education [1970] and is a retired basketball coach.)

Gary Kollman, shortstop 1966-67

Where has the time gone? The longer I think about Wyoming baseball, the more things there are to write about. Being from a farm in North Dakota, I had never ventured more than 50 miles from home. High school athletics showed me around North Dakota, and UW baseball showed me around half of the United States.
I could write about seeing and playing with my first black teammate (Jerry Marion), riding in a blue Cadillac going 100 miles per hour, walking to the front of the chow line at Camp Pendleton and Pearl Harbor or learning a new definition for the term "don't swallow the olive," but I am going to write about my senior year of 1967.

The season had more lows than highs. We never got outside before going to Arizona, and the wins were few and the losses many, the batting averages were low and the earned-run averages were high. Even the temperatures were extreme—hot down south and cold in Laramie. One game in particular stands out. We were playing Fort Carson in a night game at home. The temperature was in the 20s and so was the wind speed.

Bud Daniel gave us new wool Army surplus underwear, but we were still slowly freezing to death.

I remember this game because there were four people in the stadium. They were the announcer, *Branding Iron* sportswriter Phil White, and two Wyoming co-eds. The girls wore their ski clothes, climbed into sleeping bags and wrapped themselves in blankets to keep warm. This game could have been the ultimate low, but it turned out to be an ultimate high for two of us. One of those girls became the wife of John Hilts and the other became my wife. Marge and I have been married now for 42 years and have three children and four grandchildren so far. Looking back now, our senior year of 1967 has turned out to have been a big success for me.

UW baseball was very good to me. The program paid for my education, allowed me to see new parts of our country and play with and against the best baseball players in the country. My one regret is that the Vietnam War prevented me from going to spring training with the Pittsburgh Pirates. It would have been nice to have had the opportunity to see if I could have made it to the "Big Show."

I am so grateful to Daniel for giving me the opportunity to be a Cowboy baseball player.

(*Author's note:* Gary Kollman graduated with a Bachelor's Degree in Education in 1968 and his better half, Marge, received her Bachelor's Degree in Arts & Science in 1968.)

To my dear friend Bud Daniel for whom I have growing affection and respect.

Milward L. Simpson.

Bud Daniel chats with longtime friend Milward Simpson at the U.S. Senate Office in 1962.

CHAPTER 4

From Stockings to the Series

Baseball is a numbers game. One of the reasons why it's called America's national pastime is because fans love to look at the statistics in record books and compare today's players to those of other eras. Wyoming's baseball history dates back to at least 1921, but there aren't any official records—at least any that legendary UW coach Bud Daniel can find (and he has searched and searched for them)—of Cowboys baseball before 1938.

Milward Simpson, the legendary U.S. Senator and Wyoming Governor, is the only athlete in the history of UW athletics to be named captain of the baseball, basketball and football teams. Simpson's best sport was baseball. He played professionally on a team in Cody and had offers from some big league teams, but his father persuaded him to attend law school at Harvard, instead of chasing his field of dreams.

"When dad talked about things, even in his 90s, he said he had dreams of running in the outfield," said Milward's son, Alan Simpson, who also became a U.S. Senator. "He was a centerfielder, and I would say that was his sport. Baseball was his first love."

Oliver Knight—who became a well-known geologist in South America and later returned to Wyoming, driving his car in the Cowboys' spring trip caravans for many years—was on the 1921-22 UW team with Simpson.

"My first recollection of Cowboys baseball is of standing with two gentlemen (Simpson and Knight) in

\lled Daniel. "It was 1951, and we were
\vo historic photos on the walls of the new
! was intrigued by the uniforms the men
.. wearing. The stockings were rolled high on the
knees. This was very unusual for the time, so I asked
why they were wearing them that way.

"Simpson told me that a well known player in
professional baseball had told them to use that method
to prevent injury while sliding. Actually, he had
misunderstood the information, and the socks were to
be rolled below the knee. This was the start of a
wonderful discussion of the old days and my
introduction into the true history of UW athletics."

Paul Fitzke, a pitcher for the 'Pokes in the early
1920s, received a call up to the Cleveland Indians on
Sept. 1, 1924. Bob Linton, another UW player, was a
catcher for the Pittsburgh Pirates during the 1929
season.

The final Wyoming baseball media guide, published
prior to the 1996 season, began keeping track of the
program's year-by-year record in 1938. Dean O'Conner
was the coach that first official season and guided the
'Pokes to a 2-6 record. He was 17-24 as the skipper
from 1938-41.

Ev Shelton—the brilliant Hall of Fame basketball
coach who led Wyoming to eight NCAA Tournaments
and a national championship in 1943—coached the
baseball team in 1942 and '43 (the Cowboys were a
combined 2-10 over that two-year span). There was no
baseball at UW in 1944 or 1945 due to World War II.

On May 17, 1946, a new baseball field east of Dray
Cottage on Lincoln Highway in east Laramie was
dedicated.

Bill Bearly (3-6 in 1946), Frank Conley (11-6 in
1948) and George Cafego (10-4 in 1950) all coached the
Cowboys with Shelton (10-6 in 1947, 6-6 in 1949) filling
in the gaps.

Athletic Director Glenn "Red" Jacoby, who had committed to building a football powerhouse at Wyoming, solidified the baseball program by hiring Daniel prior to the 1951 season.

Daniel's record was 19-20 over his first three seasons, before guiding the Cowboys to three consecutive Skyline Conference championships (1954-56) and the program's only appearance in the CWS (1956).

*Art Howe, Bud Daniel and Gary Cowan catch up during the
1992 Alumni Game at beautiful Cowboy Field.*

CHAPTER 5

Majestic Cowboy Field

On April 27, 1963, Wyoming dedicated a state-of-the-art stadium complex that included a gorgeous ball park, known as Cowboy Field.

The weather at 7,200 feet was an issue the UW baseball program had to deal with throughout history, but on those rare spring days when the sun was shining and the thin air was still . . . well, there simply wasn't a more beautiful venue or setting to watch college baseball.

"There was nothing better in baseball," said former Cowboys standout Mike Mulvaney, the program's all-time leader in hits and RBIs. "When I was coaching at (Colorado School of) Mines, I don't know how many times I sat in my dugout trying to envision Cowboy Field instead of the field I was on."

"Those days when it was 70 degrees, and the wind wasn't blowing out and the fans were packing the place . . . there was not a better place to play."

The 'Pokes also started playing in the Western Athletic Conference in 1963. UW was in the North Division with BYU and Utah, while Arizona, Arizona State and New Mexico comprised the South Division.

On the field, UW finished with a 9-21 record during a rebuilding season. Off the field, Head Coach Bud Daniel—who missed the 1962 season after being recalled into active duty with the Wyoming National Guard—was elected president of the American Baseball Coaches Association and selected by the NCAA as the first commissioner of the Summer Collegiate Basin League, located in six cities in South Dakota and Wyoming.

Led by Daniel, the Cowboys remained on the national map after appearing in the College World Series seven years earlier.

At the 1963 ABCA banquet, Daniel was able to land U.S. Senator Milward Simpson, a former UW baseball captain and Wyoming's former Governor, as the keynote speaker.

"I was thrilled to have my dear friend as the speaker. I met Milward in the lobby of the New Yorker Hotel before the event. He was dressed immaculately in a full tuxedo, not realizing it was not a black tie affair," Daniel recalled. "I assured him I would immediately answer his request for a Scotch and water."

Lee Eilbrecht, the ABCA executive director, thought the cocktail party was getting out of hand considering the group's limited budget. Thinking that Simpson was the maître d', he forcefully told the Senator to "shut that damn bar down immediately."

Simpson gracefully continued sipping his Scotch and agreed to do so.

"I quickly slipped off to the head table and moved the seating so that Simpson and Eilbrecht were seated next to each other," Daniel said. "You can imagine Eilbrecht's red face as Simpson started his speech. He said 'I've been a dedicated Cowboy baseball fan and once captained the team. This is my first big-time coaches affair and I've learned that it's tough as hell to get a drink here.'"

Beginning in 1964, Wyoming's non-conference schedule—already played on the road—started getting even more difficult. Daniel's longtime friend and rival, Arizona State coach Bobby Winkles, started bringing national powers like Michigan and Oklahoma down to Tempe to toughen his Sun Devils up for WAC play.

"This gave us the same opportunity to play these teams on our spring tour. Wyoming Baseball gained national prominence immediately," Daniel said. "Recruiting brought about the availability of more experienced prospects. It also became more difficult in ways."

The 'Pokes were 18-24 in 1964 and 16-22 in 1965. They were third in the three-team North Division for the first three years of WAC play. But in 1966, after surviving a brutal spring schedule—which included games against Arizona, Michigan, Nevada-Las Vegas and San Diego State—UW (26-25 overall) won the Division.

Arizona beat Wyoming in a playoff for the Conference title and a trip to the College World Series. Cowboy shortstop Gary Kollman and pitcher Barry Johnson made the All-WAC team.

In 1967, UW opened the season at the prestigious Riverside National Tournament with a 4-3 victory over UCLA, coached by the legendary Art Reichle, one of Daniel's best friends. The Cowboys also beat Washington and Yale, but lost to Riverside, BYU, Mississippi and NCAA champion Ohio State.

The Cowboys then boarded a U.S. Air Force MAC Transport plane for a flight to Honolulu for a week-long Armed Forces Tournament. Jim MacDonnell pitched UW to a win over Army, and Brent Foshie followed with a win over BYU before the team lost nail-biters to Hawaii and Navy.

In 1968, Daniel welcomed the final recruiting class that he would coach through their senior season. The talented group of freshmen included Bill Stearns, Matt Sterling, Rick Corbin and Neal Kalberer. Returning lettermen that helped the 'Pokes to three consecutive second-place division finishes from 1969-71 included Jim MacDonnell, Brent Foshie, Ev Befus, Bob Sporrer,

Art Howe, Tom Michel, Butch Simonini, Steve Warren and Doug Weber.

Daniel left UW with a 326-363 (.470) record over 20 seasons, a remarkable feat considering the Cowboys played two-thirds of their games on the road and routinely challenged the nation's top programs.

Despite a lonely existence on the UW campus these days, Cowboy Field still has the look of an elite college baseball facility. The beautiful backdrop, highlighted by the evergreens beyond the outfield fence and the Laramie Range in the distance, remains unchanged.

"I think if they put some time and effort into it, it would be just gorgeous," said former UW star Greg Brock. "It would be one of the best parks around. With the trees fully grown, the setting is just great." (1)

Every spring, longtime UW Sports Information Director Kevin McKinney, an avid baseball fan, longs for those glory days at Cowboy Field when a rival like BYU or Colorado State would arrive on the high plains for a three-game series.

"It was the best place in the league to watch a game," McKinney said. "Wyoming had the premier yard. It had a lot of charm."

Located on Willett Drive, just east of War Memorial Stadium, Cowboy Field—which has lights, a grand-stand, a press box, covered dugouts and its amazing outfield dimensions (360' x 410' x 360')—is still used from time to time for youth baseball games.

"It was a tremendous home field advantage. I think teams came in there just petrified of the altitude, the wind, the weather . . . and I think our guys at times really took advantage of that," said Bill Kinneberg, UW's coach from 1986-92. "But despite the elements, it was always surprising how nice that field was."

Cowboy Field was the house that Daniel and the great Wyoming teams of the 1950s built and where the 'Pokes were at their best from 1963-96.

Added Kinneberg, "When we finally got home after playing 25 or 30 road games to start the season, it was always a real comfort to put on those white uniforms and play at Cowboy Field."

Bud Daniel, Wyoming coach, 1968

CHAPTER 6

Of Coors Beer Busts and the Coach

Larry Hurley, outfield 1963-64

I graduated from a very small high school with 14 in my senior class. Getting to go to Wyoming and play baseball was beyond my wildest dreams. I look back on those experiences as the best of times.

Prior to arriving at UW I played baseball at Indian Hills Community College and was a successful hitter. How Bud Daniel had knowledge of me, I'll never know. I had a letter from Daniel but thought my grades were too marginal to go to UW. I was very distraught and decided to call the coach. Somehow, after our conversation, he was able to get me admitted on probation. Evidently my coach in junior college told Daniel I was 6' tall when I was actually 5' 7" at the most. During my first meeting with Daniel he took one look at me and said: "Six-feet tall, huh? Ha!"

Coming from an elevation of 300 feet to 7,200 feet was very different. At the first practice Daniel almost killed me with wind sprints. My baseball fundamentals were way behind, but I could hit the ball. I'm certain Daniel was frustrated with my overall ability. He thought I had the wrong shoes, switched my infielder's glove for an outfielder's glove and made me wear glasses (I didn't believe I needed glasses, they bothered my hitting). I also hated the fiberglass handled bats that stung your hands so bad.

On the way south one season we stopped to play a junior college team in Pueblo, CO. We thought we were studs, going to Arizona to play the big boys. The lefthander they threw was faster than anyone we would see in Arizona or New Mexico. He blew us down and also our confidence.

Our trainer, Johnny Omohundro, saved a shortstop's life, as he was choking after a collision with an outfielder at Grand Canyon College. Omohundro also worked on a victim after an automobile accident near the ballpark at BYU in Provo.

I remember playing against Arizona State's Rick Monday prior to his move up to the major leagues. Monday also made a circus catch of a ball I hit as it was leaving the park—he was good! Getting a base hit off of Sterling Slaughter, who was leading collegiate pitchers in strikeouts at the time, was another great moment.

(*Author's note:* Hurley graduated from UW with a Bachelor's Degree in Education in 1964. He coached for 14 years and then took over the family farm.)

Jack Johnson, pitcher 1962-66

Many of my favorite Wyoming baseball stories involve Tom Woodmansee. One time while we were in Arizona, Woodmansee and some other players had driven to Mexico in Tom's dad's station wagon and were late starting back for bed check. I think Tom was driving in excess of 100 mph when the highway patrol pulled him over. He had to drive all the way back to the border and appear before a Mexican judge. Tom did not have enough cash and finally convinced the judge to accept a check. They were late and missed bed check, and the next day they were not allowed to dress for the game. Tom was scheduled to pitch and was really hot. He placed a phone call home and stopped payment on the check.

The next year we were playing Arizona in Tucson and were staying in the bunks below the football stadium. Being an early riser, I was lying in bed, wide awake, and had a direct view to the outside door. When it opened, in walked a very large Arizona Highway Patrolman, who sees me lying there awake. He walks over to me holding a game program and asks if we have a pitcher by the name of Tom Woodmansee. Being a very helpful and honest individual, I escorted the officer over to Tom's bed, where he was still asleep. I will never forget the look on Tom's face when the officer woke him up. He doubled the fine and demanded payment in cash. The officer also had a good laugh over the incident. Tom didn't think it was very funny.

(*Author's note:* Johnson graduated from UW with a Bachelor's Degree in Education in 1966. He became a football coach.)

Tom Woodmansee, pitcher 1964-65

In 1964 I was the only player on the team that did not get a base hit the entire year. I was a true Lefty Gomez (New York Yankees) type of hitter. During a tight game at Grand Canyon College, assistant pitching coach Bob Tedesco suggested to Bud Daniel that I could bunt. Coach listened to the advice, and I promptly lined into an inning-ending double play. It's too bad we did not have the DH rule back then.

That same season while playing at New Mexico, Daniel yelled for Tom Wilkinson to warm up in the bullpen. At that time, Wilkinson was sucking on a snow cone and eating a hot dog. He did not get into the game.

Our first baseman, Mike Hulbert, would always throw his infamous knuckleball back to the pitcher after a throw to first base. That drove Coach crazy, and he told Hulbert if he did again, his butt would be going to sit on the bench. Two innings later, he threw it back straight and the ball went over the third baseman's head. Coach put Hulbert on the bench.

I do believe in 1964 I was the only pitcher in all of college baseball to lose two games in a third of an inning. That happened at Arizona State after a rain out in a game the previous day that finished in a 2-2 tie. I was selected to finish that one inning of the rained out game, quickly picking up a loss. After a short intermission, I started the next game and was down 5-0 with only one out in the first inning. Hard to figure an ERA when you do not have a complete first inning.

We had fun, played some good teams and learned a lot during my days in the Cowboy program. They were times I will never forget. And baseball made me study in college so that I could stay eligible to play.

(*Author's note:* Woodmansee earned a Bachelor's Degree in Education from UW in 1966 and became a business executive).

Chuck Clare, infield 1959-62

As a sophomore in 1959, I was elated to make the team that was chosen to go Arizona for the spring practice in Tempe. When Bud Daniel gave us the itinerary for the trip I was even more excited to learn the first night we were staying in Las Vegas. Wow! I would only find out later that it was Las Vegas, NM. The two places actually have very little in common.

When we were seniors a bunch of us went out in Tempe to have a little fun and maybe even drink some beer. After all, we were missing "9-Mile." We went to one of the local establishments and ordered a pitcher of Coors. Shortly after we paid for it, the waitress came to our table with a note. I read it first. It was from Daniel, saying that we had better not drink the beer and, further, we should get out of there ASAP. Moral of the story: Don't drink where Coach does.

I remember a game at Air Force in which I hit two home runs, something I rarely did. After the first home run, which was early in the game and important in the score, as I returned to the dugout there was no reaction—no 'Way to go, Chuck,' or 'You got all of that one,' or even a 'Hum Baby.' I was wondering what was up. Then I looked at Daniel, and he was really laughing, and I knew he had told the rest of the team to ignore me when I returned to the dugout. It was a great lesson in humility.

(*Author's note:* Clare graduated from UW in 1962 with a Bachelor's Degree in Education and is a retired educator.)

Gus Angelos, outfield 1948-52

My parents were immigrants who arrived in this country looking for a better life. My dad was born and raised in Greece; my mom was born in Germany and immigrated as a young girl. Together they had a combined eight years of schooling and neither spoke English. When my dad did get a job in a restaurant, he worked 18 hours a day and 365 days of the year. We never went as a family on a vacation, to a movie, restaurant, picnic or anything like that. We did eat Thanksgiving dinner together, but not at Christmas. In that regard we were a dysfunctional family because my dad was always working. My mom had poor health. We didn't have a car or much else. Consequentially, we played outside doing sport activities and using our imaginations.

I was born in 1929 and raised in the Great Depression and World War II. I always wanted to become a fighter pilot, but missed out, being a little too young. In high school I was the leading hitter in baseball every year, and we won the state championship in Utah. Education was never a high priority in our family. My brother was the first one ever to graduate from high school. I even had a scholarship to go to Utah State for football but didn't take it. I was playing baseball in a semi-pro league with Keith Bloom and George Simms, who both played for Wyoming. Out of the clear blue sky I received a letter from George Cafego offering me a tuition scholarship for baseball at UW. Keith had written Ev Shelton, who had been the baseball coach, about me. I knew nothing about the letter.

I had two weeks to be in Laramie and did some quick soul-searching. College was never a big thing in our family growing up, but I had matured and decided I needed to go, not knowing if I could pass any classes and without preparation. Coach Cafego got me a job at the *Pi Phi* Sorority House, and I received two meals each day, which helped me survive my first year. I was totally on my own at age 17, and money was always a big problem. My family never was able to help me financially with any of my schooling, but I got by and had a lot of fun and obtained my goal of an education.

Our games were almost always played in the wind and, very often, with poor weather conditions, including snow. Crowds were small. It was really great to go to Kirkland Air Base for two weeks in the spring. One story I remember when playing against the Air Base Team. We played them two games and, in the first game, a buddy of mine hit a home run and beat us. The second game, I hit a home run and beat them. We really had a good laugh and a good time together on that one.

During my three years on the varsity, I was the top hitter two years, and Tom Bournellis beat me by a few points the other season. My batting averages were .391 as a sophomore, .412 as a junior, and .399 as a senior. During my last year I even lucked out and hit three consecutive home runs against Ft. Warren. I liked that because they really had a good pitching staff of former minor league players during the Korean War.

The good old 7,200-feet elevation in Laramie, with plenty of wind at your back, always made the ball travel. I remember one time when we had two men on and no outs, and Bud Daniel gave me the bunt signal, which I missed. I hit a home run, and Coach was still fuming about it. I wasn't a real home run hitter, but I think I led the team each year in home runs. I loved my years in college. After graduation I even had three offers to play pro ball.

I decided to go into dentistry after two years (that is another story—how an orthodontist put braces on my crowded teeth for free and talked me into going into dentistry) and was the only person in all my classes that never had any high school chemistry, physics or advanced math. Trying to study in the athletic dorm was something else. Daniel excused me from some practices so I could take science labs.

I became friends with Alan Simpson and his father, Milward Simpson, who was President of the Board of Trustees and wrote a very nice letter of recommendation to help me get into dental school. I saw Alan at my 50-year reunion and thought I was his long lost brother the way he treated me. Alan spent a lot of time in my room because he really liked my roommate, John Peters. Paul Carlin was a roommate of mine for a quarter, and he became the Postmaster General of the United States for a couple of years.

As a senior, I was elected President of the "W" Club and became a member of the Student Senate. I even made *Who's Who in American Universities and Colleges* in 1953.

Life has been very good to me, my wife Pearl and our family. I have great memories of Wyoming, and Daniel was always a very good person and a good coach. I thank him for that.

Gene Domzalski, infielder 1956-58

Early in 1958, my sophomore year, I was rehabbing an injury when Bob Devaney informed me that he planned to keep me out of spring football so my knee could fully heal. I asked him if I could go out for baseball, and he gave me permission. My life dramatically changed.

The baseball team was working out each night in the Fieldhouse in preparation for the annual spring trip to New Mexico and Arizona. Being able to face major competition like Arizona, Arizona State and Michigan was a great motivator to make the travel team. Making the two-week trip, along with a side trip to Mexico, was absolutely great.

I can remember our team as fiercely competitive and never backing away from a challenge. I distinctly recall one contest we had at home plate when we were playing at New Mexico in Albuquerque. Four of the largest Cowboys were back-to-back against most of the New Mexico football team from the stands, going at it. Finally, the state patrol cars arrived to see what was going on. In the aftermath, in the New Mexico training room, the only Cowboy being treated for a cut was Bud Daniel, who had already received the Purple Heart in WWII.

I can honestly say that Coach significantly shaped my life by giving me the opportunity to play for the

Cowboys. He also lined me up in the summer of 1958 to play for Yankton, SD, in the Basin League. That experience led me to a bonus contract and six years in the New York Yankees organization.

After my playing career was over, I returned to UW to complete my degree requirements. Daniel created a coaching position with financial aid that greatly eased our time there. It was my preparation at the University, along with Bud's direction, that led me to a successful career in college coaching and administration in Pennsylvania.

(*Author's note:* Domzalski earned his Bachelor's Degree in Education from UW in 1964 and a Master's Degree at Wilkes University, where he became Dean of Men, in 1972. Daniel said Domzalski was the last football player he ever received from Devaney).

Frank Goodie, third base 1955-56

I have always considered Wyoming's appearance in the 1956 CWS as a great achievement, as we only had 16 players on our roster while the other teams had 25 players suited up.

The young men making up the 1956 team were no different than other athletes when it came to their appetites. They liked food and plenty of it. One of Omaha's great restaurants during the 1950s was Johnny's Steak House, and it was the site of our Sunday afternoon dinner during the week we spent at the College World Series. The buffet menu featured great rib-eye steaks with Omaha's famous prime beef.

In the meantime, busboys in white shirts and black trousers removed the dirty dishes and made sure that coffee cups and other beverages were continuously refilled. Pete Kutches, one of our members who also happened to be wearing a white shirt and black trousers, was returning to his table after his fourth or fifth trip to the buffet when he was beckoned by an elderly lady who wanted a coffee refill. Pete told the lady that he was a patron rather than a waiter or busboy. She apologized after telling Pete that she had him confused with the help since he had passed by her table with such frequency. Even after all these years some of us team members still ask poor Pete to bring us more coffee. Who knows? Maybe he missed his true calling.

One of the funny stories that I recall occurred in 1955. We were headed back to Laramie after winding up our southern trip having played Arizona, Arizona State and New Mexico. We were scheduled to play two games against the University of Denver before returning to Laramie. Our living quarters for this two-day stay was the beautiful Shirley Savoy Hotel, which has since been demolished and replaced. I was assigned a room with Kutches, our leftfielder. In the evening after the first game, I joined Bob Jingling, Bob Sullivan and Don Napierkowski and went to a movie. My roommate joined George "Bud" Nelson and a few others in a beer bust in our shared room. Since Nelson had a relative who worked for Coors Brewery, the guys had access to beer at a cheap price. Obviously, quantity was not a problem for my beer-drinking teammates.

When I returned from the movie and entered the room, I thought for a moment that I had entered the bar. There was an overwhelming odor of beer and a great number of empty beer cans strewn around the room. I recalled hearing Daniel talk about a bed check, so I knew I had to act quickly. I gathered all the cans and carefully placed them in the closet on the floor up against the wall. I remember it was a large walk-in closet, and the beer can design went around the entire perimeter. When I finished, it looked rather nice and neat.

After finishing the placement of the cans, I made it into my bed just before Coach came in the room. Pretending to sleep I heard Daniel say, "That damn Kutches. I will have him running wind sprints for a week!" After this utterance he left the room. I escaped getting any blame, which was fair, I thought, since I was only involved in trying to protect my roommate by tampering with evidence.

Danny Adair, outfield 1966-68

Frank Gavin and I signed up for Bud Daniel's handball class in the fall of 1966. We were playing doubles with Coach and his partner, Wyoming athletic director Red Jacoby. I will admit that Coach was a very good handball player. Being left-handed, I took a ball off of the back wall and fired it toward the front wall. It hit Daniel square in the butt. Coach froze, turned around and just shook his head, standing in the middle of the court. The look on Coach's face scared me to death. Frank said to me as we walked back to the dormitory, "I hope you are here next semester." He was dead serious.

In the spring of 1967 we were in Salt Lake City for our annual series with Utah and BYU. We stayed downtown in the vicinity of Temple Square. We were eating all of our meals at Harry Louie's Chinese Restaurant, which was located on State Street on the second floor of the building. Daniel had met Harry when playing in the Pioneer League in 1948. All of the minor league players ate at Harry Louie's because the prices were right.

On one particular morning, the team had gathered for breakfast. As boys play pranks on one another, that morning was no exception. The "Billings" group always outnumbered everyone else. I noticed where Doug Weber was sitting, and without him knowing what I was

Pictured from left to right are Gary Kollman, Bud Daniel and Jerry Marion in the Cowboy dugout during the 1967 season.

about to do, I unscrewed the lid on a pepper shaker. This would suddenly pour pepper all over his food. Coach came into the room and sat down right next to Doug. Need I say more? He picked up the pepper shaker and every ballplayer in the room froze. Yes, the pepper covered Coach's food. Daniel shouted up to God a few times and then looked around the room. I did 'fess up to the prank. I was scheduled to start in right field that day . . . it didn't happen.

(*Author's note:* Adair earned a Bachelor's Degree in Aeronautical Science from UW in 1968 and became an airline pilot.)

George "Bud" Nelson, utility 1955-56

I remember the many hours of practice time Bud Daniel devoted to improving our skills and learning the techniques necessary for mastering the game. Having had the opportunity to coach American Legion and lower-level baseball teams, I diligently included most of the drills in my programs.

The trip south Daniel included in the preseason schedule during spring break was a brilliant strategy. Having the opportunity to practice indoors during the cold days of spring put us weeks ahead of our opponents. It was a countless number of strategies such as this one that earned a coach from a state without a high school baseball program, a very short playing season, and with only limited financial support, a place in the Baseball Coaches Hall of Fame.

Traveling to the different sites for competition, especially the trip down south with Dave Herwitz and to the College World Series with Ev Shelton, was a real pleasure. On the way to Omaha, Daniel had us stop for a quick snack at some little Nebraska town. Vic McElroy ordered fried chicken, which took a considerable amount of time. This was not to the liking of Shelton. He read the riot act to Vic, saying to him that we only wait for "stars." Looking at me he also added, "Remember, Nelson, that includes batting practice pitchers." It was exciting to have Shelton with us and for him to catch batting practice, which was a remarkable feat at his age.

I was a team member that spent very little time actually playing. The memories I have to share consist of the behind-the-scenes baseball activities—practice, pre-game and coaching the bases. Like most youngsters, I would have preferred playing a bit more, but I quickly realized that with such a talented group of returning pitchers, my chances of participation would be limited. Anyway, I enjoyed being a member of the team and really appreciated what Daniel did for me and the UW baseball program.

After I joined the coaching ranks I realized the very important role of the backup players in an athletic program. How important it is for them to challenge starters to become better players each and every day.

Thinking back to the preseason workouts scheduled at the Fieldhouse, I remember the assigned task of crawling below the portable basketball floor and between the pillars or posts supporting the floor to gather baseballs that had been tossed or hit there during practice. Although I had previously worked in an underground mine, I still became claustrophobic and very much dreaded when it became my turn to go after the balls.

On game day, I was assigned the job of hitting fungo fly balls to the outfield during warm-ups while Daniel was running infield practice. What I remember about this task was that it allowed me to finish each of the practices by hitting a ball out of the park. I always used a beat up ball so it didn't cost the university much.

Often times I have been ask what I accomplished as a player. I could truthfully tell them that I was the only player on the team that had hit a ball out of each of the ballparks we played in during the 1956 season.

Several years after my collegiate baseball experience ended, I became a teacher and coach. One of my early assignments was coaching an American Legion team. Having witnessed the outstanding successes posted during Daniel's tenure at UW, I quickly decided that it would be wise and beneficial to follow his plan of attack. Coach taught me to be prepared, to learn and follow a well-organized plan, to set goals, to have courage of my convictions and to be a positive person. America knows Daniel was an excellent coach. Records indicate and support that conclusion. What really matters is that Daniel is a great individual, loved by all former players. That's why so many Cowboys are still anxious to attend any gathering where Daniel is in attendance.

(*Author's note:* Nelson graduated from UW with a Bachelor's Degree (1957) and Master's Degree (1962) in Education and is a retired teacher and coach.)

Bob Schildgen, first base 1951

I came to Wyoming in the fall of 1948 as a football candidate, who also hoped to be able to play baseball. The general intensity of Bowden Wyatt's football program was structured in a way that the large number of candidates would in essence eliminate themselves from the program through the competitive aspects of the sport. Unless each of us could remain productive, the University simply had no intention of honoring our athletic scholarship status.

Coming down to the last week of the football season, several of us had entered into the showering area. I felt that a staff member from the Physical Education Department (Dr. Everett Lantz), whom I had not officially met, was observing us rather intently, much like he was looking for a particular individual. I somehow felt that his attention was directed at me, but nothing was said, so I went about my business drying off. This situation repeated itself the following day. Surprisingly, the gentleman approached me as I was leaving the shower room. Without a proper introduction, all he said to me was, "Schildgen, have you ever wrestled before?" I replied, "No, sir!" He then said, "Well, would you like to learn how?" Not hesitating or even thinking, I told him, "Yes, sir!" Up to this point, all of my athletic endeavors were team-oriented, and while I had hoped to be able to compete in both football and baseball at the university level, committing myself to the individual sport of wrestling would require a greater learning curve to be successful.

Fast advancing to my junior year, immediately after the wrestling season ended, I was obligated to report to the spring football sessions, which had already started a couple of weeks back. I was still harboring the thought of playing baseball, knowing full well that I had to receive Wyatt's blessing in order for this to happen. After contributing to UW's success in football and wrestling for three years, surely he would grant me such consideration if I were to ask once again. Taking everything into account, Wyatt did reconsider my request and finally consented to my participation in the baseball program, that is, with certain built-in parameters. I would be expected to fulfill my full commitment to the football program and, only after each practice session was terminated, could I report to the baseball fields. This would then most often involve my taking batting practice while still dressed in football gear *sans* the shoulder pads.

The baseball staff, consisting of head coach Bud Daniel and assistant George Cafego (also an assistant football coach), had been aware of my desire to try out for the baseball team going back to my freshman year. When I initially practiced with the team and attempted to throw a baseball, I was embarrassed by the fact that I couldn't even throw the ball from first base to home plate on a line. Daniel suggested that I should practice throwing the ball on one bounce between the bases in order to retrain my arm and shoulder muscles in deference to wrestling strengths. It was akin to redeveloping my baseball skills from scratch following a four-year layover. Evidently Daniel was pleased enough with my progress and efforts on the field and at batting drills, that he named me as a member of the Varsity squad.

I accompanied the baseball team down to Albuquerque for a string of spring training games against both armed service and college teams. We departed Laramie in the early evening via an over-the-road Continental bus, bent on driving through the night nonstop to arrive in the early morning. Shortly after breakfast and getting settled into our motel rooms, Daniel called us together for the start of two-a-day workouts. He designated me as an outfielder originally, although he intended to utilize me as a first baseman on occasion. Following a couple of intra-squad games, I started our first official game as the left fielder and hit a triple against the Lackland Air Force team based in San Antonio, TX, where my brother, Art, was stationed at the time. During the spring trip we relaxed at a nearby restaurant specializing in "broasted chicken." The place became our favorite for a couple of reasons: they served warm, soft dinner rolls, with lots of honey, and second, we could select tunes on their jukebox. At this particular time, Fats Domino's No. 1 hit, "Blueberry Hill," was playing over and over, to our delight.

Returning to Laramie, all of our remaining games were scheduled against Conference opponents. In our last game in Fort Collins against Colorado A&M (now Colorado State University), I hit a three-run homer, with a former high school teammate in the stands without my knowing it until after the game. Wyoming ended the season with a near-even record, and I was awarded a varsity letter in my only year of competition.

Looking ahead to graduation from the University of Wyoming, the uncertainty of active duty in the U.S. Army kept me and the other senior ROTC students in a state of bewilderment. Our anxiety was finally released about one month prior to being commissioned, upon being notified that our orders had been executed for an immediate call up to active duty. Three months after completing the Infantry Officer's course at Ft. Benning, GA, I was sent to Korea, where I saw line action as an Infantry Platoon leader in the Korean War and was awarded the Combat Infantryman's Badge.

(*Author's note:* Schildgen earned a Bachelor's Degree from UW in Education in 1952 and a Master's Degree from the University of Chicago. He is a retired educator.)

Bill Beck, pitcher 1959-60

I remember it simply as "The Catch." We were playing Colorado State in Laramie at the end of the season and needed a win to cinch our Division. It was very late in the pressure-packed game, and we were leading 3-2. CSU had runners on first and second with two outs. Joe Netherton was playing second base, Fred Answine was playing first base and I was pitching.

The batter hit a hard ground ball between first and second. Joe got to the ball and knocked it down, but then he hurried his throw to first. Fred threw right-handed so he had his glove on the left hand. Joe's throw was hard, but low and wide right. Instead of trying to get his glove around to catch the ball, Fred stuck out his bare hand and snagged the hard throw for an amazing catch and the final out.

The spectacular play saved the game from being tied. Cowboys win!

(*Author's note:* Beck earned a Bachelor's Degree in Geology at UW, a Master's Degree in Engineering at Arizona State and an Master's Degree in Business Administration from Oklahoma State. He is a retired Lt. Colonel, USA and university professor.)

Art Howe, Wyoming infielder, 1967-89

Bill Ewing (1974-76) had a .405 batting average and a 2.45 earned-run average during his brilliant Wyoming career.

CHAPTER 7

From the High Plains to the Big Leagues

Growing up on a farm in Eagle, ID, about 20 miles west of Boise, made Pat House tough. Certainly tough enough to pitch without fear at 7,200 feet.

"Laramie did not bother me weather-wise or altitude-wise," House said. "It was cold, and I could have had a better breaking pitch somewhere else, but I was used to hard springs."

House was pitching for Boise Junior College (now Boise State University) at the Junior College World Series in Grand Junction, CO, where he was named to the all-tournament team, in 1960 when Wyoming coach Bud Daniel approached him about playing for the Cowboys.

"I went home and did some research on the University of Wyoming. I was into engineering and when I looked at the program I said, 'This isn't too shabby and the baseball program is OK,'" House said. "Without even visiting the University, I committed to them."

House arrived in Laramie in the fall of 1960 and was the ace of the 1961 Cowboy team that won the program's fourth Skyline Conference title.

Floyd Bero, Jim Carothers, Jack Herrod, Mark Meka, Cliff Osborne and Mike Rawson were also on the 1961 team, which was one victory away from making it to the College World Series. UW lost a heartbreaker to Northern Colorado in Laramie, with a trip to Omaha on the line.

"They went, and we went home. It was very disappointing," House said. "I came into the game in relief, and I believe we were tied or one run ahead. I threw a fastball that was hit down the line and hit the chalk, allowing them to go ahead and win."

During that season, House played one of the finest games Daniel witnessed in his 20 years of coaching at Wyoming. House pitched a one-hit shutout against New Mexico in Laramie and provided the game's only score with an impressive home run as the Cowboys prevailed 1-0.

"It was one of the best games in Wyoming history," Daniel said. "Pat pitched a one-hit shutout, and he hit a towering home run that almost hit the house that was beyond right field at the old ballpark."

According to Daniel, the Lobos also had a solid club that season and threw their ace in, what has to be, the greatest pitching duel ever witnessed in Laramie. New Mexico's baseball record books don't have any information about the 1961 campaign.

"New Mexico had one of the best pitchers in the league, and I knew I had my work cut out for me that day," House said. "We went at it tooth and nail. I always took pride in swinging the bat. He threw a slider or maybe a cut fastball inside, but it wasn't inside enough, and I hit a home run for a 1-0 win. That was a really satisfying game."

Daniel took a leave of absence from the UW baseball program in 1962, House's senior season, after being recalled into service with the Wyoming National Guard. Former Cowboys great Bob Jingling, a two-time All-American shortstop, coached UW to an 11-15 record that season. Daniel returned in 1963, as the Cowboys joined the WAC and opened Cowboy Field.

"I liked Bob, but I sure wish I had old Bud for my senior year," House said.

After running out of eligibility, House still needed to complete one more semester of course work to graduate with a degree in mechanical engineering. UW athletic director Red Jacoby personally paid for him to return in the fall of 1963 and finish. With a degree in hand, the talented lefthander decided to play professional baseball with the comfort of knowing that he had an engineering career to fall back on if things didn't work out.

House became one of the few University of Wyoming baseball stars to ever make it all the way to Major League Baseball. He was drafted by the Milwaukee Braves in 1962 and, after toiling in the minor leagues, he pitched for the National League's Houston Colts during the 1967 and 1968 seasons.

House made his big league debut on September 6, 1967, against the San Francisco Giants. He threw a perfect inning of relief, and the first batter he faced was Hall of Fame slugger Willie McCovey. After the 1968 season, Houston traded House to the Cincinnati Reds just as the "Big Red Machine" was getting fired up.

"I was loaned to the White Sox and ended up playing with Indianapolis in the American Association," House said. "In the spring of 1970, I went to spring training with the Reds and made it to the final day."

The final spot in the rotation came down to House, who was 29 at the time, and a 19-year-old rookie named Don Gullett.

"Gullett could throw pretty darn hard, and they took him. I went back down to Triple-A," House said. "I could see the writing on the wall."

After 10 years of professional baseball, House decided it was time to put his UW degree to work. He is the owner of an engineering company in Boise.

Paul Roach, an assistant football coach at the time, was the one who recruited Art Howe out of Pittsburgh, luring the future Major League Baseball player and manager to go to school in Laramie. At the time, Lloyd

Eaton was building a powerful football program that top prospects from around the country were interested in being a part of.

"I came out for a visit and kind of made a commitment because I was so impressed with Paul and the way he conducted himself," Howe recalled.

Howe's dad and brother accompanied him from Pittsburgh to UW during the recruiting process. Stepping off the train in Laramie was a shock for all of them.

"When they said we were now arriving in Laramie, Wyoming, we said, 'Where is it?'" Howe says with a laugh. "It looked like a little bus depot. We stayed at the Travelodge downtown and watched the team workout. It had been nice during the spring in Pittsburgh, and we weren't dressed for Wyoming weather.

"I remember it was a beautiful, sunny day but still freezing cold. And my dad had the same hairline on his head I do now, which is not much of a hairline at all, and his head was turning blue."

When they returned to the hotel, Howe's father asked him if he was absolutely sure he wanted to go to school at UW. Art never balked.

But before graduating from high school in 1965, Howe suffered a slipped disc in his back. During his freshman season at UW he had to go to the infirmary and was in traction.

"The doctor told me if I hurt my back again I could forget about sports. Period." Howe said.

The injury would change Howe's life forever because it led to his decision to focus on baseball. Daniel made room on his roster for Howe, but couldn't offer him a scholarship for room and board until his second semester.

"My father was a truck driver and, if I hadn't gotten a scholarship, I couldn't have stayed much longer," Howe said. "I loved baseball and decided it was the way to go."

Howe, like most former Cowboys, remembers the early-season trips down to Arizona and New Mexico as the best of times, even when high-powered teams were getting the best of UW on the scoreboard.

"Those trips were a lot of fun, and the competition was outstanding," Howe said. "The problem was it was our first time outside and Arizona State's record would be some crazy numbers like 18-0 or 20-1. And we'd just be walking outside the Armory for the first time."

During the 1969 season, Howe's senior year, UW opened up with a brutal schedule that included games against Arizona State, Michigan and Oklahoma, all in one day. The 'Pokes endured a 12-game losing streak before winning five of six WAC games and putting themselves in position for a Conference title. Howe played hurt throughout the entire campaign.

"I remember the first game my senior year was against Arizona State. Larry Gura was pitching against us. I beat out a ball at first and tore a thigh muscle and didn't know it at the time," Howe said. "As time went on, that muscle started rolling up my leg. I didn't want to miss my senior year so I kept playing. It looked like I had a softball on the front of my leg, but we taped it, and I got through the season."

Wyoming, battle-tested from the spring trip, put a winning streak together down the stretch and positioned itself for a WAC title entering the final game against BYU. The 'Pokes and Cougars split the first two games of the three-game set at Cowboy Field.

"In the last game they scored a couple runs against us, and the wind started blowing straight in, and we were finished," Howe said of UW's 12-0 loss on May 17, 1969. "It wasn't in the stars that we were going to win the Division, but we played great baseball that season."

Howe figured that was the end of his baseball career. He underwent surgery on his back and leg, graduated from UW with a degree in Business and started a job as a computer programmer for Westinghouse. But after healing up, Howe—an All-WAC selection in 1969—started to play baseball again for a semi-pro team. A friend of his called all of the Major League teams to see if they would be willing to give the former Cowboys standout a tryout.

"The Pirates were the only team with a tryout left. They had just opened Three Rivers Stadium," Howe said. "I went to the tryout at the age of 23. Most of the kids were 16-to-18. Evidently, I did all right. After the six-hour workout, they called off three names, and mine was one of them."

Interestingly, another future Major League Baseball manager, Ken Macha (Milwaukee Brewers), was one of the other names called.

Howe signed his first playing contract with his hometown Pittsburgh Pirates in 1971. He played all four infield positions during an 11-season career that also included stops with the Houston Astros and St. Louis Cardinals. Howe played in 891 games with a lifetime batting average of .260, with 43 home runs. He is better known as a steady and highly respected big-league manager for the Houston Astros, Oakland Athletics and New York Mets.

"From time to time, when I would be playing or managing, people would yell, 'Art, I went to Wyoming,'" Howe said. "Wyoming fans are very loyal."

Howe's daughter graduated from Wyoming and, 40 years after his senior season, he attended a homecoming reunion in Laramie.

The decision to play baseball at Wyoming was an easy one for Greg Brock.

"It was the only scholarship offer I had," Brock explains.

Brock grew up in Stayton, OR, and played high school baseball for his father Joe. UW head coach Jim Jones had some connections in the Portland area, and a scout tipped him off about a talented and unattached rural player with a sweet swing.

"It was pretty interesting," Brock said of arriving in Laramie and signing a letter of intent to play for the Cowboys from 1976-79. "It was more of a shock learning that I had a scholarship offer. I think it had been turned down by a couple of other players before coach Jones offered it to me. . . .

"Being on the West Coast, I wasn't knowledgeable about Wyoming. It was definitely different, but now this is my favorite part of the country."

Brock developed into one of the finest hitters the Cowboys ever sent to the plate. He was an All-American selection his senior year and owns the UW records for hits in a season (86 in 1978) and career doubles (57). He is second all-time in career hits (251) and walks (95).

In 1978, the Cowboys finished 35-24, the most wins in program history at the time. Kirk Harris (catcher), Joe Ewing (outfield), Earl Lawson (infield), Mike Lusardi (outfield) and Felix Oroz (pitcher) joined Brock as All-WAC selections during his career at UW.

"We were very competitive, and we had some good talent," Brock said. Both Ewing and Oroz made it all the way to the Triple-A level professionally. "It was a really unique group. There were eight or nine other freshman, and all but one or two went to Wyoming for the whole four years."

As Brock's impressive collegiate career was winding down he started thinking about beating the odds again and making it in Major League Baseball.

"I was a very realistic person, and it was my junior year when people said, 'You could get drafted,'" Brock said. "After my junior year it became a goal of mine to get to the next level. I didn't get drafted until my senior year. After that my goal was not to get stalled anywhere along the way."

Fort Lewis Rangers, 1962.
Major leaguers clockwise from
left: Tony Kubek (Yankees),
Derron Johnson (Oakland),
and George Thomas (Boston).

Bud Daniel and Bruce
Haroldson together
with the Ft. Lewis
Rangers, 1962.

After putting together a brilliant high school and college career in obscurity, Brock was thrown into a pressure-packed situation as a rookie for the Los Angeles Dodgers in 1982, replacing the legendary Steve Garvey. Brock spent five seasons with the Dodgers, appearing in two National League Championship Series, and five seasons with the Milwaukee Brewers before retiring with a lifetime batting average of .248 and 110 home runs.

"I was very thankful for the overall experience I had in Laramie," Brock said. "Because I wouldn't have had the career I had if not for Wyoming. I grew up there."

Brock lives in Loveland, CO, where he built a very strong baseball program at Mountain View High School. His younger brother, Eric Brock, played baseball at UW from 1979-82. And his son Danny—who was a senior first baseman at the University of Saint Louis in 2010— probably would have strongly considered becoming a Cowboy had the program not been dropped in 1996.

"I thought Wyoming ran one of the best programs when you consider what they had to contend with as far as the weather," Brock said. "It's a little bit sad when you see some of the northern schools in the Big Ten have baseball, and Wyoming doesn't."

Jeff Huson felt right at home during his recruiting visit to Wyoming. It was a sun-splashed spring weekend and the co-eds were sunbathing as they would be in his native Arizona.

"When I first transferred up there I didn't have a winter coat. The first time I flew into Laramie it was about 75 degrees," Huson said.

Huson committed to UW and drove back to Laramie in the fall of 1983 to finish his collegiate career after two successful seasons at Glendale Community College.

"Driving up on Route 287 between Fort Collins and Laramie, I crossed into Wyoming and looked to the left and saw snow on the peaks," Huson said. "It was August. I thought to myself, 'Oh no.'"

Despite the weather, Huson thrived in the Cowboys program under Jones. The smooth infielder earned All-WAC honors in 1984 and 1985 on 'Pokes teams that combined for 38 wins and 63 losses.

"I just remember it was a lot of fun playing at home because we got good crowds," Huson said. "People would come with their blankets and things to drink inside those thermoses, and that was fun."

Believe it or not, Major League scouts weren't exactly flocking to Cowboy Field. Huson didn't really get discovered until he began spending his summers playing on a semi-pro team in Beatrice, NE, painting houses in his spare time to keep himself afloat financially. After two years, Huson finally got a break and was signed by the Montreal Expos in August 1985. He attended spring training in March of 1986 and was sent to the minor leagues to play rookie ball in the Expos organization with about 30 other players.

"In Nebraska I got a lot of exposure against other college players and guys with good talent. After my senior year, six or seven scouts finally called me," Huson said. "I went back to Beatrice expecting to be there two or three weeks and it turned into two or three months before signing in late August of that year."

Huson ground his way through Single-A, Double-A and was eventually called up to the show on September 2, 1988.

"My biggest moment playing baseball was getting to walk out on to the field in the Majors for the first time and the awe of it," Huson said. "I thought to myself that if I never got to play another game, I had made it. That overshadows everything."

Huson played in some historic games during his 14-year career in Major League Baseball. As a member of the Texas Rangers from 1990-94, Huson was on the field for Nolan Ryan's sixth and seventh career no-hitters.

With one out in the ninth inning of Ryan's seventh, and final, no-hitter, Huson, the Rangers shortstop, had to scoop a slow-roller hit by Rickey Henderson and gunned the speedy all-time steals king out by a step at first base.

Nolan said, "Nice play, Huey."

"As I was going back to short, the only thing I could think was, 'Oh, God, don't let them hit the next ball to me,'" Huson recalled. "That's when the magnitude of it all hit me."

After the 1994 season, Huson was traded to the Baltimore Orioles, where he played for two seasons, including the game when Cal Ripken, Jr. broke Lou Gehrig's "Ironman" record for consecutive games played. The former UW star played third base when Ripken broke the record. Huson was the first person to shake the hand of the Hall of Fame shortstop before he made his famous postgame circle around Camden Yards.

Huson married a Cheyenne girl and now resides in Denver, working as a television analyst on the Colorado Rockies broadcasts.

Ralph Vaughan, Wyoming pitcher, 1955-56

CHAPTER 8

Surviving War and Bad Umps

Mike Cooke, outfield 1957-60

In the spring of 1960, we were playing Colorado State in Fort Collins. I must have walked to get to first base since a lefthander was pitching, and hitting lefties was not my strong suit. Bud Daniel gave me the steal sign, and I took off on the first pitch. The catcher's throw beat me to the base, and I made a "classy" slide right into the Aggie fielder's glove, which was between second base and me.

The umpire was right there and called me out. I would have been if Tom Hartley held onto the ball. It was now firmly under the left cheek of my butt. I shouted to the umpire that I was safe, as Hartley had dropped the ball. The umpire repeated the call, "Out!" Now I was multi-tasking because Hartley has his hand in my crotch feeling around. I swatted his arm telling him to get his hand out of my crotch, at the same time yelling at the umpire, "I am safe!"

After maybe 45 seconds (seemed like 30 minutes), I reached under my butt, picked up the ball, showed it to the umpire and said, "Now what am I?" He called me safe. To this day I'm upset with the umpire because he made a call without seeing the ball.

At a later date, the same umpire called me out on strikes a couple of times. He needed to get his eyes checked. We had the umpires from Denver, who regularly called our games—"Red" D'Hallicourt, Julie Carabello and Leo Ball—but this guy was the worst!

(*Author's note:* Cooke graduated from UW with a Bachelor's Degree in Accounting in 1960 and is a retired USAF and commercial airline pilot.)

Peter Kutches, outfield 1953 and 1956

I chose the University of Wyoming athletic scholarship when they guaranteed I would be able to participate in three varsity sports. My freshman year they allowed me to play football, basketball and baseball. My sophomore year the football coaches changed, and the rules changed. My senior year I was allowed to play baseball because I no longer had spring football.

Bud Daniel gave me the opportunity to play baseball again. I remember he put me in to pinch-hit. I had not played for several years, and I don't know what happened, but I could not swing that bat. I struck out. Froze. My understanding coach made certain I played more from that day on. He was a down-to-earth coach who treated players right. I tried to emulate his coaching philosophy and techniques when dealing with my players during my coaching career.

Daniel created a sense of comfortable camaraderie among all the players, which has continued with every two-year reunion.

(*Author's note:* Kutches earned a Bachelor's Degree in Education from UW in 1956 and a Master's Degree from Western Michigan in 1968 before starting a career as a teacher and coach.)

Ev Befus, outfield 1964-68

One of the highlights during my time at Wyoming was 1966, the year we won the Northern Division of the

WAC and played Arizona in a playoff in Laramie. We didn't fare so well against the Wildcats, but it was great finishing in front of Utah, BYU, Air Force and Colorado State. We did defeat Arizona once on our southern trip. As I remember it, John Hilts pitched, and this was the last time a UW baseball team defeated an Arizona team.

Bud Daniel gave me the steal sign on numerous occasions, and I still have scars on my right hip and knee from sliding. I had a difficult time catching up to the fastball and kept bailing out on the curve ball. I regret that Daniel never could teach me how to steal first.

I never questioned any of Coach's on-field decisions. There was a time, however, when I thought he had lost it. Being a native of Wyoming, I did not have much experience driving in heavy traffic. When we traveled in University cars, Coach assigned someone to be in charge of each car and anticipated that the player selected would do the bulk of the driving and be responsible for arriving at our destinations safe and in a timely manner. I was not totally comfortable driving in Casper or Cheyenne and, when we hit Los Angeles, I was expected to do the driving. I was sure that Daniel had it in for me. Our car took the first exit, and Bobby Sporrer, who was from California, did the driving from that point on. Once Gordie Westhoff took a wrong turn on our way to Tucson, and we ended up going to Taos, arriving about 12 hours late, just in time for the game.

We had a catcher from the Chicago area, Butch Simonini. I remember when his parents came to Laramie to watch a weekend series. His mother spent most of one day preparing an honest-to-goodness Italian meal, homemade sauces and the works.

I was a good athlete in high school in a number of sports. Red Jacoby, the UW athletic director, gave me a full scholarship and told me that I could play any of the sports that I wanted. I walked into the locker room my freshman year to check out my football gear. My God, I didn't know they grew people that big. That freshmen class was the group that lost to LSU in the Sugar Bowl as seniors. I turned around and left and thought maybe basketball would be a better project. When Mike Ebberly and Gordie Westhoff got finished schooling me, I talked to coach Bill Strannigan, and he thought my decision to play baseball might be a good one.

I don't think I ever thanked Daniel enough for giving me the opportunity to play for him. Playing baseball in Wyoming, you don't see the kind of pitching that others get to see where they have high school programs. Coach's patience and encouragement were instrumental in my being able to become a contributing member to the program.

Jerry Marion and I collided in right center field on a flyball and cost us a win against Michigan. Another time, we played in a tournament at Riverside, CA and defeated UCLA, Washington State, Yale and lost 5-4 to Ohio State, the defending NCAA champions. We then flew to Hawaii for a week-long U.S. Navy tournament.

A trip to Las Vegas also stands out. I don't remember much about the games, but I do remember I had a little money set aside for the strip. We were in a line for a breakfast buffet and there were numerous slot machines along the way. I had lost all of my money before we had our first meal.

(*Author's note:* Befus earned a Bachelor's Degree from UW in Education in 1969 and is an educator and coach).

Shorty Epperly, pitcher 1966-68

It doesn't seem possible that it has been over 40 years since my days in Laramie. Being able to walk on and make the team is something I have always been very proud of. Bud Daniel gave this small-town Wyoming kid the chance to meet some people and see some places that otherwise would not have been possible.

There are many indelible memories. We were practicing in the Armory at the Half Acre Gym, with the wooden mounds and the circus net, when a hitter squared up on one. It sounded like a cannon going off. People have a hard time believing me when I tell them about that makeshift facility we used in our preparation to go on the road.

Several years ago our youngest son graduated from Marine Corps boot camp in San Diego. I related to him the story about a drill sergeant that came into the squad bay where we were staying and jerked one our teammates out of the top bunk by his hair. I think the sergeant was just having some fun with us, but it sure got our attention.

Ralph Vaughan, pitcher 1955-56

Coming to Wyoming in 1955 and seeing the caliber of players we had amazed me. In junior college I had competed against Southern Conference (Furman) and Atlantic Coast Conference (Clemson) teams and was shocked to see we had such better players at UW.

My big problem in 1955 was learning to pronounce names like Napierkowski, Knezivich and Litecky. The wind in Laramie always amazed me. Routine fly balls would go forever, sometimes out of the ballpark. We even had a 425-foot homer against the University of Denver. The wind was tough to pitch in as the curveball wouldn't break, but, boy, would my knuckleball flutter.

Our first trip to Arizona sticks in my memory. We all got sunburned and, believe it or not, Don Napierkowski was injured when he fell out of bed—what a baby! He sure got a ribbing.

Some players' actions stick in my mind. Bob Fisher, our 1956 catcher, was a scholarship swimmer at UW. I'd always know when he was upset with me as he would walk to the mound hitting the side of his head, the way swimmers clear the water out. Fritz Heiss, the ex-football player and our first baseman, would meet runners coming down the line in a tackle-ready position. I would have to yell, "Touch the base, Fritz!" Gerry Nagle and Frank Goodie were the "old men" on our 1956 team. I always listened to and looked up to them. Bob Sullivan and Napierkowski were smooth in the outfield. I always worried about Bob's mind being on girls rather than baseball. He was quite the ladies man.

Mort Drury was a small Warren Spahn. Bob Villasenor closed his career on a high note, pitching so well in the district finals and winning at Omaha. If he had only had my control and knuckleball, he would have gone far in baseball. His death just prior to our Wyoming Athletic Hall of Fame festivities was a tragedy.

Jim "Happy" Hoppe, our second baseman, will always hold the record for the most CWS home runs by a UW player. He got one, the only extra base hit I remember him having. Who could ever forget Bob Jingling? The best college player I ever saw. He had Major League talent and was such a nice and decent human being.

Our 1956 team being inducted into the UW Hall of Fame was one of the proudest moments of my life. What an honor and one we certainly deserved.

Without baseball, I guess I would have had to spend my life working in the cotton mill. Baseball gave me an education and a hopeful outlook on life. I will always be grateful to Bud Daniel for giving me the opportunity to play for the Cowboys. God knows how I would love to live those days again, but I'll always have the memories.

Bob Bullock, second base 1969-73

My best experiences playing college baseball came while playing for Bud Daniel during my first two years at Wyoming. My senior year in high school the Coach was recruiting for his next freshman class. The Cowboys had just returned from a trip to Hawaii, and he wisely used this trip for recruiting. However, all the players that attended UW from my class never went further west than California to play other teams. He got a lot of mileage in recruitment out of that one trip to Hawaii. Many of us are still waiting for our turn. I am told I showed up my freshman year wearing my Hawaiian shirt. Wonder why?

I came to UW as a second baseman and played most of my time that year as the backup to an All-Conference player. Daniel had a philosophy that if you could hit the ball, he would find a place for you in the lineup.

Coming back from our spring training to Arizona and California, we stopped and played New Mexico. Our starting right fielder was sent home for disciplinary reasons, and I was inserted in the game. I had never played outfield in my life and remember the first ball hit to me. I had to go back to the warning track to make the catch but was hoping the center fielder would get there before me. He wasn't even close, so I had to make the play. The one thing I could remember is that my hands were shaking while I caught that ball, as I wasn't sure I had judged it correctly. When you play your entire life in the infield and then are moved to the outfield, it is a whole new experience. I am not sure the pitching staff was too crazy about me being out there.

The cardinal sin you did not want to commit playing for Daniel was taking a called third strike. One time I was called out on a ball that was truly around my ankles. When I got back to the dugout, coach didn't say a word as I spent the next couple of minutes complaining about the call. The next time at bat I got called out on a ball that was thrown right down the middle of the plate. This time he wasn't so silent. He reminded me of my complaining the prior time at bat and wanted to know what was wrong with that pitch. This time I didn't say a word.

One of my highlights came in a game against BYU during my sophomore year. I was now the starting second baseman and remember making two good defensive plays and a key hit to help us in winning the game. The next day my name was even put in headlines in the local newspaper. The real highlight, however, was when Daniel informed me that a scout for the New York Yankees, who was there to watch our captain Bill Stearns, inquired about me after seeing that game. Daniel informed him I was just a sophomore, so nothing further came of it. I never felt my abilities would ever take me beyond the college level, but for a scout to even inquire about me was extremely exciting. I had a good year in the field that season, making very few errors. A friend of mine who played for BYU said their coach, Glen Tuckett, told their players to hit the ball anywhere except at me. I must have had the respect of that opponent.

Another highlight for me was hitting my first and only collegiate home run. We were playing Iowa at the Arizona State field, and I hit one over the left field fence. Until I saw the umpire waving me around, I almost stopped at second base. I didn't know until later that all those that hit a home run during the season were treated to dinner at the Coach's house at the end of the year. Connie, Daniel's wife, was a terrific cook and made an authentic Italian dinner for us.

I must have been a better game player than a practice player. My freshman year, Daniel stated that if he had to judge my talents due to what he saw in practice, he would never have even given me a uniform.

One of the items I remember most about playing for Daniel is how he handled us as young men. He never said a word about making a physical error, but he did have talks with us about our mental errors. After making an error, he would never bring it up again at a future time unless you made the same mental error again. I always admired that trait in his coaching style.

Playing for Wyoming was an enjoyable experience, especially playing for Daniel. Being from Denver, my father was able to see all our home games and many of the away games that were played in Colorado. The conservative nature of the school, the proximity it was to my home, the quality of the baseball facility, the education I received, and the Coach himself made for an ideal situation. I am thankful I had the opportunity of playing for UW.

(*Author's note:* Bullock graduated from UW in 1973 with a Bachelor's Degree in Parks and Recreation).

Bob Sporrer, center field 1966-69

Before a game in Tucson, AZ, a 40-year-old man comes up to the dugout and says to Pat Angelovic, "Hey, we have a group of Little Leaguers who would like to meet your team after the game. What motel are you renting?" Pat answers, "Oh, we don't have a motel, we are staying under the football stadium."

After the game we get back to the room under the stadium and the guy had ransacked the room and stolen any valuables—watches, wallets, whatever he could carry. I remember the story for several reasons. First, I had taken what little cash I had out of my wallet and hid it in my finance textbook. The move saved the cash, but I still lost my wallet.

Second, that night I had missed curfew, having been out with my old buddy who was a catcher on the Arizona team. We had partied, and I made more than a little noise opening and closing my locker and getting into bed. This aggravated the coaches. First thing the next morning, Daniel read me the riot act. Coincidently, that very moment, my Arizona buddy shows up to tell me he has my wallet. He told coach that we had been chasing all over Tucson to find the guy who owned Beaver's Band Box, who had called to say he had found my wallet. He had noticed my buddy's name and phone number in the wallet.

I'm still not certain that Coach swallowed that story. However, I did start the doubleheader that day wondering if the party the night before would have any effect on my ability to see the baseball. I ended up having a great day at the plate, going 6-for-8, but I must confess that my hitting performance was enhanced by the fact that my friend crouched behind the plate catching for Arizona was telling me what pitch was coming.

Another memorable moment from that series was before the game during batting practice. Colonel Pat Murray, who we all thought was almost 90 years old and nearly blind at the time, was standing near the third base coach's box. Angelovic was slyly tossing small pebbles at the Colonel and turning the other way so he would not know who it was. After about six tosses, the Colonel said, "Hey Angie, I don't care if you throw those pebbles at me, just don't hit me in the jewel box!"

(*Author's note:* Sporrer graduated from UW with a Bachelor's Degree in Business & Finance and is in the banking business).

Dave Gossin, catcher 1956-58

As an 18-year-old, small-town Nebraska boy, I was delighted to be offered the opportunity to try out at Wyoming. The chance to play baseball and receive a college education was an offer I could not pass up.

Bud Daniel was a good mentor who worked with my talent limitations. I was not a slugger, so Coach had me use a short bat and employ a split-handed grip. I didn't have a shotgun arm, so Coach worked with me on a quick step release on throws. I was not a fast runner. Coach had no remedy for that. I was a good defensive catcher and had some experienced mentors in Ron Drost and Bob Fisher.

During the 1957 season, two games stand out. We were playing Arizona at Tucson, and they had very fast teams that used aggressive tactics, such as the run and bunt, or not stopping at second base. One steal attempt, I was able to get the call at second base. That helped take off the pressure. Later the same game, I solidly connected on a ball to deep center. The game was played on a field with no outfield fence. The center fielder took a step in, and the ball got over his head and kept rolling. As I rounded second base I tripped, fell and went sprawling headfirst into the dirt. I looked up at the third base coach, and he was giving me the windmill sign, so I got up and headed for third for a triple. I still saw the windmill sign. So I labored mightily to home plate for a dramatic inside-the-park home run.

I fully expected to be greeted with the joyous "Atta boy," but was instead greeted with a Cowboy bench in hysterical laughter. It must have been really funny because I even saw Daniel stifle a laugh.

Once we were playing New Mexico in Laramie, and it had snowed six inches after the Friday game, and on Saturday morning the snow was scooped and base paths were burned. We had to get the games played, and we needed a win. Big flakes were coming down as New Mexico loaded the bases with no outs. The next batter bunted in front of home plate. I fielded the ball, stepped on home and threw to first for two outs. The next batter hit a high pop foul back of home. I had trouble figuring out which "snowflake" to catch. I grabbed the right one for the third out, and the Cowboys went on to win.

(*Author's note:* Gossin earned a Bachelor's Degree in Education from UW in 1958 and is a retired educator.)

Frederick "Fritz" Heiss, first base 1952-56

When I arrived at Wyoming I had a football scholarship that guaranteed that I could also play baseball. In 1952, I played on a successful freshman football team and, in the spring, I went out for baseball. At that time, freshman could not play varsity ball, so we had our own team and schedule of games. Once the schedule was complete, we were on our own to finish up the scholastic year prior to going home for the summer. I was approached by Paul Petrich, our baseball graduate assistant, who asked if I was interested in joining him and a couple of other Cowboys baseball players, Herb Manig and Gerry Nagle, to play in McCook, NE, for the local "McCook Cats." This was at a time when ball-players from many colleges joined teams in the Midwest to play summer ball while working at daytime jobs to make money for the following year.

During the last month of school we went to McCook to play a game and make a decision if it would be worthwhile to play there for the summer. After the ballgame, which was played in North Platte, NE, we drove back to Laramie. On the way, near Ogallala, NE, we came up on a semi-trailer truck that was broken down and on the highway. We hit it, and I sustained a skull fracture, broke my jaw in two places and was rushed to the Ogallala hospital by a minister and his wife, who were passing the scene of the accident. After leaving the hospital and spending the summer worrying about my future at UW, I returned to school in the fall of 1953. I completed my makeup exams and found out that I had lost my football scholarship. This is when Bud Daniel came to bat for me. He worked out a decision with the athletic director Red Jacoby that allowed me to continue on scholarship to play baseball only for the rest of my time at Wyoming.

The next three years were very exciting for a young guy who only wanted to finish school while playing baseball and perhaps continue to play baseball after college, if fortunate enough. Daniel gave me the opportunity.

Being a member of the CWS team in 1956 was the highlight of my baseball career. During my second and third years I really enjoyed the friendships that I gained from the other guys living in the athletic dorm, especially when I finally learned to speak "Chicago-ese." When my bride Helen and I got back for my last year, I was pretty much removed from the dorm closeness with the other guys. We did have the freshmen (Mort Drury, John DeYoung and Pete Peterson) over for our first Thanksgiving dinner, and it was a comedy of errors.

(*Author's note:* Heiss earned a Bachelor's Degree from UW in 1956 and a Master's Degree from Troy State. He is a retired Colonel, USAF.)

Wyoming coach Bill Kinneberg (1986-92) has a discussion with an umpire at Cowboy Field.

CHAPTER 9

Cowboy Baseball A.D. (After Daniel)

After a playing and coaching career at the University of Wyoming that went from World War II into the Nixon Administration, Glenn "Bud" Daniel decided to leave Laramie and took an administrative position in the Arizona Athletic Department.

Jim Jones, an outfielder for the Cowboys from 1961-65, became the head coach prior to the 1972 season.

"My first experience in the Wyoming baseball program was the freshmen tryouts in the fall semester. The graduate assistant coach started naming players and putting them in their known positions—Mike Hulbert at first base, Fred Brigham at shortstop and so on," Jones recalled. "After he had placed those players, I realized that they were all the recruited players who probably had a lock on those positions. The Coach turned to the rest of us and asked if anybody played outfield. I immediately sprinted to right field—the only position available at that point.

"Thus began the career of one of the most 'defensively challenged' outfielders to ever to play for Coach Bud Daniel."

Jones grew up in Casper, WY, and was a product of the city's American Legion program, which later produced Major League players such as Tom Browning, Mike Devereaux and Mike Lansing.

"My first trip was an education on and off the field. Going from the Half Acre Armory to the high, clear skies of Arizona was a shock for all of us, but particularly for me coming out of Casper," Jones said. "I'm sure I was the last player selected for the trip south, and I wasn't concerned about getting into a game early in the trip."

Jones took a seat at the end of the bench as UW played powerhouse Arizona State on a picture-perfect afternoon in Tempe, AZ.

"Suddenly, I became aware that Coach Daniel was calling my name. I'm sure he had to call it several times since I never expected to be called. I thought maybe he needed some bats picked up or something," Jones said. "The game was getting close, and he sent me in to pinch hit. Go figure?"

While Jones was on deck, Hulbert was at the plate and facing Skip Hancock, the nation's leader in strikeouts.

"The first pitch to Mike hit him in the ribs and knocked the wind out of him," Jones said. "After he recovered, I had my first college at-bat. I took three quick swings at pitches that sounded like strikes and went back on my spot at the end of the bench. That was my welcome to college baseball."

Jones said that the baseball players would often sneak blocking dummies from the football program's storage rooms up into the Fieldhouse.

"We spent hours hitting the dummies with weighted bats. When they finally ripped out, we would exchange them for another," Jones said. "The football coaches must have thought their players were really hitting hard in blocking drills."

Jones, like Daniel, was very loyal to UW as the head coach. He compiled a 286-414 record during a 14-year career running the Cowboy program. Some of the players Jones was able to recruit to Laramie included former Major Leaguers Greg Brock and Jeff Huson. UW had 19 All-WAC selections during the Jones era.

In 1976, Bill Ewing broke the NCAA single-season home run record previously held by Arizona State's

Reggie Jackson as part of a devastating lineup that included his brother, Joe Ewing, and Brock.

"I enjoyed Jim a lot. He was very educated. Even going on to pro baseball he knew more skills than any coach I had in pro ball. He was a great coach for me. He believed in me," said Bill Ewing, a star in the California Angels minor league system until an injury derailed him off a promising Major League path. "We had excellent talent. He could spot good athletes. Laramie is kind of a hard draw for people, and you're not going to get the big-name players, but you can find some really good ones up north."

In 1978, Jones guided the 'Pokes to a 35-24 record with a second-place finish in the WAC's Northern Division. At the time it was the most single-season wins in program history.

"The extended travel required by the Wyoming program provided rich athletic and personal opportunities on and off the field for the players," Jones said. "I was fortunate to be included in those experiences. . . ."

"It was a difficult task preparing for competition in tough conditions and with the extensive travel, but the relationships and friendships we developed with our teammates enriched our time at UW. It is unfortunate that student-athletes no longer have that opportunity at Wyoming."

As the head coach at Texas-El Paso, Bill Kinneberg was used to beating up on the Wyoming Cowboys. Furthermore, the young coach—an Arizona native—was not a big fan of the brutally cold weather in Laramie.

Fortunately, Kinneberg listened to his athletic director at UTEP, who informed him that the Miners baseball program was going to be cut and that longtime UW Head Coach Jim Jones was leaving to accept a job at St. Mary's.

"I was kind of the only one available," Kinneberg said, when asked how he ended up as the new head coach at Wyoming in 1986. "I was still on contract at UTEP, but I really wasn't doing anything because they were getting rid of the program. My AD called me and said, 'Hey, did you see the paper today? Wyoming has an opening, and that could be a great opportunity for you.'"

"I didn't think it was the thing for me. Then I received a phone call from (UW athletic director) Gary Cunningham asking me to apply. The juices got flowing, and I went up to an interview and thought it was terrific. Three weeks later I was moving to Laramie, and it was probably the best seven years I've had."

The 'Pokes finished with a 29-19 record during Kinneberg's first season in Laramie, including a first-place finish in the WAC's Eastern Division. The accomplishments on the field in baseball only added to the amazing runs Paul Roach's football team and the Fennis Dembo–led basketball team were about to embark on.

"It was kind of a crazy set up because the WAC rotated the Division each year, and we happened to get into the weakest Division. And Jim had left some good players for me," Kinneberg said. "It was a break for me to be a coach that year and perfect timing because of the state of the athletic department. We were going to Holiday Bowls and our basketball team was in the Sweet 16.

"Things were really going well in the whole department at that time. We were getting exposure on TV, and that helped all of us."

Kinneberg, a brilliant recruiter, assembled a team capable of winning the WAC in 1990. That season, Wyoming, led by pitcher Scott Freeman and infielder Victor Vargas, established a new program record for wins (37) and came within a few outs of winning the championship. A loss to rival Colorado State, the worst team in the Conference, on the final day of the season ended the 'Pokes title hopes.

"The 1990 team was probably the best team in the history of Wyoming. We were three outs away from winning the WAC," Kinneberg said. "We had a tremendous team. We had a three-run lead in the last game against CSU, and they tied it up in the ninth inning and beat us in extra innings. That would have been a heck of an accomplishment."

The Rams only won four of their 28 conference games that season. But the upset in Fort Collins dropped the Cowboys (20-8) from first to third in the WAC standings, behind San Diego State (21-7) and BYU (20-7-1).

Longtime UW sports information director Kevin McKinney, an avid baseball fan, described the loss to the Border War rivals this way.

"When we lost to CSU, I was as low then as I've ever been after any football or basketball game," McKinney said. "We were going to win the WAC." (1)

Kinneberg compiled an impressive 212-157 record in seven seasons at Wyoming. He left to become the top assistant at Arizona State, and he is currently the head coach at Utah.

In 2009, Kinneberg led the Utes to a Mountain West Conference (MWC) title and their first NCAA Tournament appearance since 1960. With the addition of TCU to a conference that already included BYU, New Mexico and San Diego State, the MWC is becoming a force on the national scene, just like in football and basketball.

Wyoming and CSU are the only MWC institutions that do not have baseball programs.

"It's kind of sad," Kinneberg said of the demise of UW baseball. "Baseball had been played in Laramie for so long before they dropped it in 1996. There are all of the excuses—the weather, the travel—but Bud, Jim, David

(Taylor) and I really put good teams together. In 1990, we had a series with Hawaii that drew 2,000 people a game. It was wonderful. But some people had it out for it."

Jim Gattis, a wonderful baseball coach, took over for Kinneberg and led the UW baseball program in 1993 and 1994.

"If I made one mistake, it was leaving Wyoming," Gattis says 16 years later. "I loved it there."

Gattis left Laramie to tend to his growing coffee shop business in southern California. The University's flirtation with getting rid of the baseball program was also getting serious at this time. After a 19-31 finish in 1993, Gattis adjusted to baseball life at 7,200 feet and led the 'Pokes to a strong season during his second year in Laramie.

"The weather sucked, but I figured out that's okay," Gattis said. "There is no question I was deceived that first year with what I saw in practice inside the Fieldhouse compared to what happened out on the field. The next year I was better at winter training. After having six guys playing positions they weren't recruited for in 1993, we made decisions about moving players around, and I felt like we had a contending team."

Gattis helped Bo Haley change his swing, and, in 1994, he emerged as one of the nation's top home run hitters. The Cowboys were in contention for a WAC Eastern Division title until losing a doubleheader on a snow-covered field at Air Force to close the season.

"Everyone beat Air Force except for us," Gattis said. "We had the league won, dog-gone-it. That was miserable."

After Gattis guided Wyoming to a 32-23 record in 1994, the following feature story about the lovable baseball vagabond ran in the *Los Angeles Times* (2):

The wheels of Jim Gattis have seen plenty of miles. Grab an atlas, pick a page and Gattis has been there as a ballplayer or coach.

Wherever rubber meets the road, Gattis has been there: California, New York, Florida, Alaska, Canada. Lately, though, it's been one blowout after another.

Just the other day, Gattis bought two new tires for his Jeep, then blew a tire. He replaced it, then blew out the replacement.

"I think I ran over an elk horn or something this time," Gattis said.

That's entirely possible, because Gattis, 41, is the baseball coach at the University of Wyoming. He is no deer in the headlights, though, frozen in place and waiting for something to happen. As usual, Gattis is making something happen.

During his career as manager or head coach in the minor leagues and college, Gattis has won four pennants in three different leagues. Then again, a manager in the low minors could win every game and few would ever know.

Not with Gattis, though. Not since 1984, a year after noted baseball author Roger Kahn bought the Class A Utica Blue Sox of the New York–Penn League, the team Gattis managed. Kahn detailed the frenetic 1983 season in a bestseller called "Good Enough to Dream."

Colorful? Gattis was paisley. A graduate of North Hollywood High and a former first-round draft choice, Gattis hated the book for years. Made him look like a lunatic, he said. Kahn embellished too many facts and incidents, he told his friends.

Actually, Gattis called it a pile of you-know-what.

Years rolled by before Gattis again picked up the book. A lightning bolt called perspective struck him.

"I thought I got a raw deal," he said. "But I read it again a couple of years ago. You know what? It's more accurate than I cared to admit at the time."

Gattis has softened, to be sure. College players aren't paid professionals, after all. Many actually play for, ahem, fun.*

"For some of these guys, baseball's not life or death," Gattis said.

"Now listen up, everybody," Gattis said.

He was a powerful 6-footer, 31 years old, with straw hair and a remarkably mobile face. He had firm, even features and a lantern jaw and sometimes under his straw-colored hair the manager, Jim Gattis, looked like a movie version of a grown-up Huckleberry Finn.

Sometimes, when his blue eyes raged and his mouth set and his jaw jutted, Jim Gattis was a sadistic drill sergeant. He looked at his charges with equal measures of hatred and contempt.

"Baseball," he would say, "is not like life. It IS life. The games are a 3-hour lesson in life every day. . . ."

The young players were startled by Gattis' eruptions . . . certain players would wonder if Gattis' single-mindedness did not exceed the bounds of reason, and perhaps, sanity.

Gattis learned to battle, scratch and claw when he was young. His parents died before he turned 15. His brother, Rick, 10 years his senior, became his guardian while Gattis grew up in North Hollywood.

"My parents being deceased is probably why I really, really got into sports," Gattis said.

Hardship as a kid taught him to appreciate the value of a buck, too. After years of grinding out a living as a minor league coach while trying to support a family, Gattis has spent the past three years building his own little business empire.

"I'm currently a rich bastard," he said. "I was once a highly debted bastard. That I'm still a bastard is the constant."

* "One year I found out that Volvos weren't selling around Tucson, (where I lived)," Gattis said. "Not at all. But out here in Beverly Hills, the Volvo is a hot car for people who can't afford a Mercedes."

"So I borrowed some money from a friend and bought a Volvo in Tucson for $8,000. Then I drove it here and sold it for $11,000. I must have done that with six or seven cars."

—R.K.

* Gattis' chain of espresso coffee shops in Orange County—five of them, to be precise—is so successful, he doesn't need to coach. At least, there's no financial need.

"I have no desire to be a famous baseball coach," he said. "This is just about baseball."

When Gattis took over the Wyoming program in January 1993—just a few weeks before the season began—it didn't much resemble a baseball team at all.

Gattis had never managed a team that finished lower than third in his eight years of pro ball. Though the Cowboys jumped to a surprisingly fast start, Gattis was acutely aware that reality would eventually set in.

Wyoming traveled to Cal State Northridge in the spring of 1993, surrendered 44 runs and was swept in a three-game series. Gattis' eldest son, Luke, watched from the stands and wasn't getting much positive feedback from Valley-area fans, some of whom remembered his dad.

Afterward, son approached father and issued a "Luke-warm" review.

"Dad, there were some guys talking in the stands," said Luke, now 15. "They said, 'That Gattis guy used to be a good coach. I wonder what happened. I guess he's no good anymore.'"

While trying to keep a straight face, the Coach said, "Geez, give your old man a chance."

"I don't know, Dad," Luke said. "I think they might be right."

Wrong. The Cowboys finished 19-31 in Gattis' first year, but it didn't take long for him to work his mercurial magic. That spring, Wyoming turned heads across the nation by giving heavily favored Brigham Young all it could handle in a battle for the WAC East Division title.

In fact, had Wyoming swept a doubleheader from BYU on the final day of the 1994 season, the Cowboys would have won the Division title.

Gattis didn't walk away empty-handed, though. He was named the Division Coach of the Year for a team on which seven starters played out of position.

Wyoming improved to 32-23, which made Gattis a man of considerable stature in a state with 500,000 residents and one major university.

"I was infamous last year and famous this year," he said.

It's a tossup as to which he was in the minors— probably a little of both.

Gattis couldn't turn off the emotional spigot. He took each game home, ruminated on the day's successes and failures and let it eat away at him. He started as a minor league manager at age 28 in Victoria, Canada, soon after his minor league playing career sputtered to an end.

"I had pretty good instincts for the game," he said. "It was on-the-job training. I admit that I had a burning desire to win.

"I was reasonably well-prepared. Not necessarily emotionally."

* He had the managerial tools. Good head for strategy. Strong instructional capabilities. English major with an ability to communicate. A steel trap memory for the names and tendencies of the opposition. A cool head at all times. Well, maybe not the latter.

"I was a very poor loser," he said. "That can be helpful, that can be detrimental."

The Blue Sox coach, after a defeat, was sometimes blue in the face.

"Tomorrow had a lot of yesterday in it," Gattis said. "Things would eat me up. Things would terrorize me."

* The year before, 1982, Gattis had gone wild on at least two occasions when he felt the umpires were weighting their decisions against the Blue Sox. After a fiery protest got him nowhere one night, he uprooted second base, walked out to right field and scaled the bag over the wall.

On another protest, he walked to second base, took off his spikes and pretended they were hand grenades. Biting off an imaginary firing pin, he hurled the spikes in the general direction of the umpires. . . . The fierce Utica grenade thrower was given a week of enforced rest.

* Perhaps Gattis' playing career affected his temperament. He once had the professional game in the palm of his hand, but it slipped away.

As a senior at North Hollywood High in 1970, Gattis was a standout quarterback and third baseman. He was cut from the football team as a freshman at Nevada Las Vegas, however, and came home to play baseball in the spring of 1972 at Valley College.

Before long, scouts remembered the name. In fact, he was atop the talent list. The Atlanta Braves selected Gattis in the first round of the June amateur draft in 1972. The Braves dangled dollars in his face. He said, no thanks.

"I have some regrets," Gattis said. "Since both of my brothers had gone to college, they wanted me to go to college, too. I could have taken the money. Then, who knows what happens?"

What did happen, in fact, was horrific. While playing for UC Santa Barbara in the spring of 1973, Gattis was beaned in the cheek, near the eye socket.

A surgeon painstakingly pieced his cheekbone together, with the help of some wires and hardware. Teammates called him Plate Head for years, though Hard Head also would have applied.

"I was not a pretty picture at the time," said Gattis, who was sidelined for six weeks.

Black and blue became his least favorite colors. His senior year was marked by a series of nagging injuries. By the time June rolled around again, scouts decided that he hadn't improved much since his days at Valley. Gattis, who graduated with an English degree, was not drafted.

Gattis signed with an independent team with no big-league affiliation, not unlike the club he would later manage at Utica. The fiery third baseman played well—he was named the most valuable player of the Northwest League in 1978—but not well enough to catch on with a big-league organization. He retired in 1979 and was offered the managerial position with Victoria a year later.

"It was real easy to say yes," Gattis said.

Gattis' first three minor league teams finished second in their respective leagues. Gattis insists his teams had the talent to finish first.

"I had 'em wrapped too tight," he said. "They were too intense. I was too intense."

* One still, hot August afternoon, I heard my name called with great urgency. It was Gattis, who said he was worried because the team was unresponsive to his latest assortment of fight speeches.

"I'm gonna do something now that will set fire to this team's butt," Gattis said. "I'm gonna activate myself as a player. I may not run well anymore, but I still know how to hit."

"With intensity," I said.

"I'm not kidding. I want to get in this pennant race with my bat," Gattis said.

Before the season ended, Gattis inserted himself into the lineup five times. He did not hit safely once. I remember thinking that intensity alone was not enough.

Then I resolved to give the word "intensity" a good long rest over the winter.

—R.K.

* Gattis was demonstrative, Gattis was demanding, Gattis was occasionally demented. Of course, Gattis also won.

In 1987, while managing the North Pole Nicks, a team composed of college hotshots in the Alaska Summer League, Gattis decided he didn't like the overall effort during a loss to the Fairbanks Goldpanners.

Scott Cline, now the baseball coach at Camarillo High, batted cleanup for the Nicks, a team that included Eric Karros of the Dodgers and Luis Gonzalez of the Houston Astros. At the time, Karros and Cline were teammates at UCLA, playing under mild-mannered Coach Gary Adams.

When Karros and Cline learned they would be playing in the summer for Gattis, they spent an evening vigorously leafing through Kahn's book, reading passages aloud and wondering what they'd gotten themselves into.

There, in vivid detail, was the story of Roger Kahn and his coach, Genghis Khan.

"We'd heard a lot of stories," Cline said, laughing. "Gary is more low-key. It was like going from night to day."

After the loss to Fairbanks, it was midnight when the bus arrived at North Pole, and players were anxious to catch some shuteye. Not so fast, said Gattis, who called a practice.

The 'burg of North Pole is located near the Arctic Circle, land of the midnight sun. Bad news for the players—Gattis' practice didn't end until 4 a.m.

"I think we spent most of the four hours running around the bases," Cline said. "He was demanding, a perfectionist, but his way worked.

"I learned more about baseball than I had in a long time. We learned about growing up, too."

So did the Coach, eventually. After coaching at Miami of the Florida State League, Gattis served as an assistant at Pepperdine from 1985 to 1988. A wife and three kids kept his feet better planted on terra firma, too.

Dave Taylor has run across Gattis at three different stages of the Coach's career. Taylor, a 1982 graduate of Rio Mesa High, played for Gattis at Salt Lake City in 1986, then served as an assistant under Gattis in Miami three years later.

Taylor, a former head coach at Oxnard College, is now an assistant at Wyoming and can testify that change has indeed been effected.

"He has definitely mellowed," said Taylor, 30. "I think he communicates better with players now. At a lower volume. There's still a little Bobby Knight in him though."

* Like a souped-up engine with plenty of miles on it, Gattis maintains that his high-compression days are over. Evidence supports the claim.

In fact, a different team directed by Gattis was roughed up, and the Coach didn't utter a word. It was the season finale, and Gattis' crew finished eighth in a 12-team league.

"This one won't go on my resume," he said.

When the game ended, Gattis didn't rant or rave. Heck, he took the team out for ice-cream, whereupon his small army of Little Leaguers aged 7-9 mobbed him like he was Santa Claus.

Believe it. Gattis was hitting fungoes to the very same pee-wees a few weeks back when he noticed something curious. The ball went one way, the players another. Gattis spoke to his youngsters, carefully choosing his words.

"Uh, you know, you can't catch a ball if you keep running in the other direction," Gattis said, making a point to be upbeat and constructive.

Blank stares all around. Finally, from under the bill of an oversized ball cap, a kid piped up: "Yeah, but if I wait until it stops rolling, it can't hurt me."

Gung ho Gattis was speechless, believed to be a career first. What the heck could he say? After all, it was only baseball, not an all-or-nothing proposition. Message received. "I accepted it as being absolutely right," Gattis said with a laugh, "and we moved on from there."

*Two-time All-American Bob Jingling, Wyoming shortstop,
1953-55*

CHAPTER 10

Wyoming Baseball "Changed my life"

Bob Sullivan, outfield 1953-56

During my first two years at Wyoming I threw a lot of batting practice and developed a sore arm my sophomore year. That same spring some of our left-handed pitchers, who will remain nameless, were also having arm problems and spent countless sessions having their arms massaged by the trainer Doc Peterson. So when I went in to have my shoulder worked on, "Pete" started putting balm ointment on my left shoulder and began massaging. I thought this must be a new technique: Do the left arm and shoulder first and then go to the right shoulder and arm. Pete finished the left side and said: "Well, that should take care of it." I was too embarrassed to tell him I was right-handed and went into the showers without having my throwing arm and shoulder worked on. I still blame that on those nameless left-handers—Bromley and Manig!

In 1954 we were playing in the Skyline Conference championship series at the University of Montana in Missoula. We were playing the final game to win the championship, and I was playing in center field in late afternoon shadows and clouds. A ball was hit in my direction, and I broke left toward right field where Fritz Heiss was playing. Much to my chagrin, the ball landed behind me close to where I had started. There was a simple explanation—I saw a bird going that direction, and it was obviously easier to see than the baseball.

However, my teammates have never let me forget it and still laugh about it. My excuse is my imperfect eyesight and the late afternoon shadows.

One time we were playing Colorado State when a very long train was passing the ballpark. We had been winning the game, but with the loud noise and distraction, the Aggies scored a number of runs. We ended up winning a high-scoring ballgame. Once again, home field advantage made a difference.

While playing at New Mexico, the wind started blowing with gusts up to 50 mph. Finally, in the late afternoon, we moved down to the Rio Grande Valley where the professional field was located. We ended a very long day with a win by virtue of "Stormy" George Petrol, the New Mexico coach and a dear friend of Bud Daniel, who did not notice his scorekeeper had made an error. It was too late to start a big discussion. Both teams were ready to call it a day. Our eyelids felt as if razors had worked on them from the dust.

We were housed at nice hotels in certain cities like Denver, Salt Lake City, Omaha and Tempe. In Albuquerque, we stayed at the barracks at Kirtland Air Force Base and under the Arizona football stadium. Many of us did not realize it at the time, but it helped us develop comradeship, discipline needed to learn how to live and get along in tight places when we entered the military later.

(*Author's note:* Sullivan, a retired Colonel, USAF, earned a Bachelor's Degree from UW in Business Administration in 1956.)

Joe Glenn, outfield 1963-65

The first fall team practice was in Wyoming's old Armory. There was not a lot of room for practicing.

When Bud Daniel addressed us without a smile, we were told, "I will do all the smoking and drinking for this entire team."

We had a formidable group, from California product Don Cadman to 5-7 Larry Hurley, a dedicated Missouri farmer, to a couple of Wyoming cowboys and one American Indian. We were scheduled to run ten 100-yard wind sprints for our first real workout. After seven sprints, Coach mercifully called a halt as only three of the players were still standing. All of us felt the effects of the 7,200 feet of altitude on the Laramie plains.

As an innovative mentor, Daniel had us work out in the snow with orange baseballs. They were easy to see, especially in the Armory. Our bats were encased in fiberglass handles in order to save the expensive Louisville Sluggers. Coach didn't pull any punches when we were preparing to go to Arizona on an extended trip. He said, "Prepare to get your butts handed to you morning and night." This turned out to be the truth. We left Laramie at 25 degrees with Johnny Omohundro, our trainer, planning for several bottles of baby oil, the sunscreen of the day. We were booked on a DC-3, affectionately call the "vomit comet." Most of the players had never flown and were startled when we landed in 85-degree heat in Phoenix.

Arizona State had already played 25 games and was ranked nationally. Bobby Winkles had a formidable lineup, with future Major Leaguers such as Sal Bando, Rick Monday and Reggie Jackson (yes, the same Reggie Jackson who would become known as Mr. October with the New York Yankees). Daniel showed great composure and restraint as the competition was very tough. Even before I started coaching, I realized this was a classic example of his determination.

It takes a lot of study for student athletes to make up assignments on extended trips. Naturally, we signed out for the "library" in Phoenix. It was used by many of the out-of-state athletes. It was roomy, air-conditioned and well stocked with cold beverages. I learned much there, including how to cozy up to a sleek, tan "she-devil," as opposed to roping a pale cowgirl in ski clothes.

One of my favorite stories involves a retired Army Colonel (Pay Murray), who always traveled with us. He was a spry, silver-haired, 80-year-old master storyteller who constantly entertained the players. He taught us how to slide back into first base after taking a sizable lead off the bag. He bunted better than half of our club and loved a good pepper game. He couldn't turn his head because of military injuries. Each year he drove a new white Cadillac with cruise control. On our way to Arizona, south of Denver on I-25, he was driving 75 mph with the cruise control on. A sudden distraction to the left caused him to turn his entire body to the left. The Caddy responded by going into the median. Murray, who was not wearing a seat belt, tried desperately to hit the brake pedal. It was a wild ride until one of the players reached the ignition key and turned it off. It was unanimously decided that Daniel would become the driver of the Cadillac the rest of the way.

We were playing Arizona in Tucson at Hi Corbett Field, where the centerfield fence was a 40-foot solid monster. When you are playing there you can't gauge or feel the wind. We were ahead 3-2 in the bottom of the seventh. Don Cadman, better known as "bat man," was pitching a masterpiece. Arizona had runners on second and third with two outs and the cleanup hitter hits a knuckleball toward me. It moves in the 20 mph wind coming over the monster fence. I moved one way, and the ball moved again the other way. I thought about sliding. Knowing that Cadman was pitching the game of his life, I made another move forward about a half a step, the ball dives to the right, I lunged and make the catch. Back to the dugout where Coach says: "Why the ballerina move? Are you trying to give me a heart attack?. . . Nice catch."

Back in Laramie, we had snow daily while waiting to play BYU. We finally went to Cheyenne to play the game. I was coaching at third base and picked up their signals immediately. Coach let me relay the pitch to the hitter using the last name. We scored 10 runs until I yelled, "Jonesy" to Jim Jones. He promptly hopped up two steps in the box and hit the ball out of the park. BYU then realized what was happening. My roommate and best friend, Larry Hurley, had two home runs, one from each side of the plate, in the same inning. That has to be a record. We won 13-12.

I want to thank Daniel for allowing me to play the game I truly love. I wish I could have hit better, but I gave my best. He helped me into teaching and coaching, and as a result I was very successful. I married a girl from Wyoming, have two successful children, coached basketball for 12 years and returned to UW as assistant coach to Jim Jones in 1978-79.

Bill Lutz, pitcher 1959-62

I was 17 years old when I arrived in Laramie, and it was my first time away from my home in Illinois. A friend of my father's dropped me off in front of the Wyoming Motel. I called Bud Daniel and he said, "There is no room at the Inn!" I stayed across the street from the motel at a place called the Paper Palace. I called my dad and told him I wanted to come home right away. He told me to give it at least one day.

The best year I pitched at UW was my sophomore year, when I made the All-District team and pitched in front of Mort Drury, John Phillips and Herb Manig. I learned a very valuable lesson from Daniel when I did not receive my first semester scholarship my senior year. I thought I was too good and did not pay attention or workout, as Coach had directed me to. It was a blessing in disguise to learn the lesson of always giving 100 percent and never taking anything for granted. I want to thank Coach for that. I'm certain the percentage of Daniel's players who graduated was very high.

The entire time that I pitched at Wyoming, if I was in a tough situation and needed a strikeout or a batter out, I heard, "Lutz, bull your neck, bull your neck!" I knew the term meant—get tough, challenge the batter, gut it up—but I had never heard it said that way before, nor had my teammates. We still laugh about it today.

I was pitching a game in Greeley, and my fiancée (now my wife) came to watch. A pitch was hit off me to dead center field, where Norm Sagara was playing. I looked out, and Norm just disappeared over bushes and hedges. A minute or two passed, and he finally came out. Norm to this day tells me I should have been more worried about him flying into the bushes for a ball that went over his head for a home run.

On our southern trips each spring we received $5 a day for lunch and snack money. One year we had Sagara's Chevrolet, and five of us piled into that car. Colonel Pat Murray always was one of the drivers in our caravans. Riding in his Cadillac was great as he constantly entertained us with great stories or card tricks. At 80 years of age, he taught us how to slide back into first base, usually while wearing his good brown slacks. None of us will ever forget that.

In one game at Arizona, I was lucky enough to hit two home runs. As a result of that feat, the next game I started in right field. I almost was decapitated trying to catch a fly ball I misjudged completely as it went for a home run. That was the end of my career in right field.

Another great memory came at an ABCA convention when Daniel, his wife Connie, my wife, Sue, and I all enjoyed dinner and many stories with Tom Lasorda at Carmines Restaurant.

(*Author's note:* Lutz graduated from UW with a Bachelor's Degree in Education in 1961. He went on to earn degrees from Northwestern and Northern Illinois and is a business executive).

Herb Manig, pitcher 1952-55, 1957-58

The wind was howling like only a spring wind in Laramie can. The diamond on the old field faced the southwest, and the wind was screaming directly from the west. I don't recall the team we were playing, but Ron Drost was catching, and I was pitching. Ron called for a curveball to a right-hand batter. I nodded my agreement, took my windup and threw as hard as I could, keeping pressure on my middle finger and snapping my wrist downward as I threw. On any other occasion, an accurate hard, left-handed curveball would curve in and down to a right-handed batter. So imagine my chagrin when a powerful gust of wind caught my pitch and sent it so far in the opposite direction that the umpire called it a ball.

We were to play New Mexico State at Las Cruces. The stadium announcer began calling out the starting lineup for Wyoming, butchering the multi-syllabic names of the players of southern European descent that Bud Daniel had recruited from the steel mill section of Chicago.

One of the reasons I was eager to come to the University of Wyoming from Chicago was because I had read too many Zane Grey novels, and I became enamored of the West even before I got here. I did not have any transportation, but that did not stop me from walking miles east of the campus, hunting for the elusive rabbit, spotting antelope and deer and marveling over what caused the tortured landscape.

Soon I met up with a UW swimmer from Cheyenne, Dick Miller, one of the finest backstroke performers in the country. He and I became best friends. And he owned a car. So we spent many happy hours cruising the Wyoming backcountry, hunting and fishing. One day we went out west of Laramie and began fishing on the Laramie River. I knew that we had baseball practice that afternoon, and it was also the day for our official baseball team photo. Yet we focused our attention on the fishing.

Dick had waders and had worked himself over to an advantageous location on the river. He yelled to me to try to fish off the point where he was, but it was on the opposite side of the river. So Dick came back to me, ordered me to get on his back and we started wading across the river. Just what caused Dick to start giggling right in the middle of the river I don't know, but it was contagious and quite soon both of us were laughing our heads off for no good reason. While still in the middle of the river, Dick lost his footing and started falling backward. Instead of releasing my legs, he simply held on to them so that when we went down, I went down clear to my head.

Now, much more sober (and cold and wet), we realized that I needed to be at practice. I was going to be late for the team photo. At the Fieldhouse, I opened the outside door and began walking down the hallway to the locker room. There he was! Coach Daniel really looked fierce. But as we walked closer toward each other, I noticed his expression changing until he took full stock of his frightened player, soaking wet clothing and water still squishing out of his shoes with every step. Now he appeared more amused than angry and said, "Just what in the hell happened?"

I think Daniel realized that this was just what he had to tolerate when he recruited an immature, left-handed pitcher.

(*Author's note:* Manig graduated from UW in 1958 with a Bachelor's Degree in Education. He is a retired Farm Bureau Executive and has moved back to Laramie.)

Jack Hall, pitcher 1956

My one year with the Cowboy baseball program was a wonderful experience in my college career and my life. A memory that stands out more than any of the others was our road trip to start the 1956 season. We had very little time outside for practice, but the amount of quick experience was not long in coming.

We played in Colorado, New Mexico and Arizona. In addition to the collegiate baseball teams, we also played two United States Air Force teams. When we arrived in Tucson, AZ to play the University of Arizona, we learned their record was already 25-0. If that doesn't shake a team's confidence, nothing will. It did not shake up the Cowboys. Bud Daniel's leadership made me realize numbers mean nothing if you are tough inside as well as the outside. You have to play as one group of athletes, one team. It was that inspiration that led us to the College World Series in Omaha.

(*Author's note:* Hall graduated from UW with a Bachelor's Degree in Education in 1956 and coached baseball and football for many years. He is now retired.)

Jim Hoppe, second base 1954-58

The year was 1954. I had just become only the second of the four brothers in my family to graduate from high school. My parents did not come to the ceremony. I was looking at a future of working in the corner convenience store owned by my older brother. My father delivered furniture in the Chicago area, but most of his money went to support the neighborhood tavern. It didn't seem bleak, because it was the only lifestyle I knew.

Then Bud Daniel offered me a scholarship to attend Wyoming. No one in my family had ever been to college. Two of my brothers didn't even make it through high school. However, since it was the best of the options I had at the time and offered the chance to play baseball, I packed my bag and headed to Laramie. For a guy who had never been west of Milwaukee Avenue, this was a giant leap of faith. I had many second thoughts, beginning when I got off the train at the station in Laramie. Grade-wise, I was on probation the entire first semester of my freshman year. The academics were hard, but my other option held no promise, so I got busy with the books and got myself off probation. The baseball at UW was the love of my life, and I was thrilled with the success of the team. I will always be proud of being a part of the only UW team to ever be invited to play in the CWS in Omaha.

I graduated from UW in 1958. My parents did attend that ceremony. I went on to obtain a Master's Degree in Education Administration from UW in 1968.

I married a Wyoming girl—a decision I made while looking out the window of the athletic dormitory. My entire career was in Wyoming. I was a physical education teacher for 10 years in Casper and an elementary principal for 21 years. After 31 years in the Casper school system, I retired to enjoy our five children, all graduates of UW. Six of our 12 grand-daughters are in college and the rest know they will go to college. It is expected in the Hoppe family.

When we visit Chicago, I see my brothers and their children and grandchildren. They are still eking out an existence in the city. Most are high school dropouts.

They work at temporary, menial tasks for minimum wage.

The scholarship to Wyoming that I received in 1954 not only changed my life, it gave my family and generations to come a great life, too. There is no way to put a value on that!

Mark Meka, infield 1960-61

My favorite Wyoming memory is from 1960 against Arizona. We had lost in Tucson, and the Wildcats came to Laramie later in the season to play a doubleheader. They were highly ranked with several All-Americans, including catcher Allen Hall. I remember they came into the dorm with their navy blue blazers with the University of Arizona crest before the game. It was very impressive.

We played a great game and beat them in the opener. It was very special to me because when they beat us in Tucson earlier, the fans were terrible. My dad even got into it with the fans in the stands. I met with Arizona's coach after the games in Laramie, and he congratulated the team and me for playing well. It was a great day for all of us.

(*Author's note:* Meka graduated from UW with a Bachelor's Degree in Education in 1963 and later earned a Master's Degree from Arizona State. He is a retired educator and coach).

Pat Thorpe, outfield 1958-59

One cold, windy day our pitcher was having trouble retiring the side, and I began throwing small rocks at him, bouncing them to the mound and telling him to throw strikes. Finally, we made three outs and headed into the dugout to get warm. We went three-and-out in about five minutes. As we returned to the field, Bud Daniel told me to go pitch and that he would throw rocks at me. When I went to the mound, Coach put Buddy Bishop in to catch. The other team probably thought that two midgets escaped from the Shriner's Circus. The only thing we didn't come out of was one of those small cars. But we probably won that game.

Another memory that stands out from the 1959 season was a game against New Mexico in Laramie. They had brothers playing for them, the Unterbergs, and I think they were twins. One of them hit a long drive to right center, he was sure it was going to be a home run, even though right field was very deep. I heard Norm Sagara call from right field, "I got it." That's all I needed to hear. I took off to the dugout. When I crossed second base, Unterberg was still running and saw Norm make the catch. Unterberg stopped and said to me, "Damn, six feet more and I got a home run."

I told him he would have had to hit the ball to Cheyenne, and Norm still might have made the catch. He was mad as hell.

(*Author's note:* Thorpe played two years, leading the club in hitting both seasons. After the second season he decided that all the classes he had taken would prepare him to enter business with his father. The Cowboys wished him well, and he was very successful in the business world.)

Barry Johnson, pitcher 1964-66

I came to Wyoming from Minnesota, 50 miles north of Fargo, ND. The weather in that part of the country is well-known. So when the guys would complain about the weather in Laramie, I would tell them it was the "banana belt" compared to my home.

We had some characters on the team. Mike Hulbert, known as "Flaky Jake," would never throw the ball back to the pitcher normally. It was always a knuckleball. In the evening he would sit for hours, rub his baseball bat with a bone and talk to it. This procedure would smooth the bat and enable him to be a good hitter. I guess it worked for him. Gerry Thompson, our team captain, would carefully tie a shoestring around the handle of his bats. Why? I do not know. He suffered a severe ankle sprain in a game at Arizona State and missed half of the 1965 season. He caught a spike sliding into home plate.

While at ASU, Jerry Marion and Hub Lindsey were lying around at the motel pool covering themselves with big white towels. When several of us saw that, we asked why? They replied that they did not want to get sunburned. They ignored the fact that at 7,200 feet in Wyoming they could really get sunburned. The team did go through several bottles of baby oil as sunscreen.

From 1964-66, Arizona State had some notable players like Sal Bando, Rick Monday and Reggie Jackson, all future Major League stars. During one game, Bando hit two rocket shots over Gordy Westoff's head at third base. I called Gordy to the mound and told him to move in a couple of steps as Bando would probably bunt this time. Gordy instead moved back three steps, and Bando hit another shot right at him.

The 1966 season turned out to be special with a 52-game schedule that included ASU, Arizona, Michigan, San Diego State and UNLV. We finished the southern trip with a 9-12 record. After playing regional schools, we headed into our Conference schedule. We managed to take one game at BYU and Utah in the tough three-game road series. When BYU returned to Laramie we took two of three from them, which meant a sweep of

Utah would give us the WAC Northern Division Championship. We won all three games (6-3, 16-3, 4-3). Gary Kollman, Ev Befus and Jerry Marion were All-Conference selections. Arizona beat us for the WAC championships.

(*Author's note:* Johnson earned a Bachelor's Degree in Education from UW in 1966 and is a retired coach and teacher.)

Ron Salvagio, utility 1961

Although baseball at the University of Wyoming never worked out the way I would have liked, I will always be grateful for the scholarship and opportunity. Being from a middle-class family, the financial support allowed me to be the first person in my entire family to attend college. The other positive thing was that Bud Daniel introduced me to Wyoming and its great University.

I enjoyed my undergraduate years at UW and graduated with a B.S. in Accounting. After three years as an officer in the Army, including a year in Vietnam, I returned to the University and obtained an M.S. in Accounting. I am now retired and play a lot of golf, but have always stayed connected to UW. I have had the pleasure of serving on the Board of the Art Museum and have been a member of the Foundation Board for several years.

It was great fun to play with guys like John Van Allen, Jim Jones and Mike Hulbert. They were not only teammates, but became good friends. One additional note: my son was seriously considering playing for Wyoming when it discontinued baseball, which we all believe was a mistake. He went on to play at the University of South Alabama.

Bob Jingling, shortstop 1951-55

I was born and raised on the southeast side of Chicago. During my senior year at Bowen High School, we had a very good baseball team. We won the South Side Division and were playing the North Side Lane Tech, who had won the North Division, at the University of Chicago's Staag Field.

After the game, our coach, Harry Pritikin, called all of the senior players to the outfield and introduced us to Glenn Daniel, the head baseball coach from the University of Wyoming. We were all fired up. I can remember Daniel saying: "Play well, and good luck."

We had won the first game 5-0 and went on to play Chicago Vocational High School at Comiskey Park, home of the Chicago White Sox. We lost a squeaker, 3-2. Two weeks after graduation, I found myself working at U.S. Steel as a ladle operator. I was very depressed because I felt there was a big world out there, and I wanted to explore the possibilities and did not feel I would be able to do it. Little did I know Daniel would give me an opportunity to realize my dreams.

When I returned home from the 7-3 shift one day, my mother told me Coach Pritikin had called, and I called him back immediately. He asked me if I remembered Daniel, who wanted to know if I was interested in attending UW on a full baseball scholarship for four years. He took our entire infield, and we won three Conference championships in four years. They were the best years of my life.

From 1951 to 1955, I had to take Air Force ROTC to stay in school because of the Korean War. I graduated from UW with a Bachelor's Degree in Accounting in 1955. In November of 1955, I was called to active duty in the Air Force. I completed pilot training (F-86) and made a career in the USAF, retiring as a Lt. Colonel.

Jeff Huson takes a big swing at Cowboy Field.

CHAPTER 11

The Cowboys' Hit Kings

Bill Ewing had many great afternoons on the baseball diamond from a standout career in the Rapid City, SD, American Legion program to making the game look pretty easy at every stop in the California Angels organization. Fittingly, a memory that stands out in the legendary Wyoming slugger's career was a picture perfect spring game between UW and Colorado State in Fort Collins. Ewing blasted three home runs and just missed out on a fourth round-tripper against the rival Rams in 1976.

"We played a game in Fort Collins where every pitch looked like you were playing backyard wiffle ball. Both teams were in great moods, and everybody was having a lot of fun, even the coaches," Ewing recalled. "It truly was like a sandlot game . . . I hit three homers in a row and the football team for CSU was behind the fence watching to see if I could get another one. The pitchers were getting more intense as the game went on, and it was kind of like batting practice.

"On my fourth at-bat the pitcher threw one right down the middle, it was the fattest pitch I had seen, and I popped it up to the first baseman."

That '76 season, Ewing broke the NCAA record for home runs in a season with 23 (in only 53 games), while hitting .428 and driving in 66 runs. The home run mark had previously been held by a former Arizona State standout with a familiar name—Reggie Jackson.

Ewing, an All-WAC selection in 1975, played on some of the most exciting teams in UW history, including three seasons with his brother, Joe Ewing, an All-WAC selection in 1977. In 1976, Greg Brock was also in a potent 'Pokes lineup, as was All-Conference catcher Kirk Harris.

"Other than shoveling snow over the fence (at Cowboy Field), I really enjoyed it," Bill Ewing said. "I loved the field and the fans. We had some very loyal fans and we had some years where we were competing well and a lot of people came out to see if we could break some of the records."

Bill Ewing holds UW's single-season records for doubles (21), home runs (23) and total bases (176), marks all set in 1976. He is also second all-time in career batting average (.405), third in doubles (50), fifth in home runs (32) and has the program's best career earned-run average (2.45), after making some relief appearances when the bullpen was overtaxed.

Joe Ewing owns the program's single-season (37 in 1977) and career (79) records for stolen bases.

"I wanted to play for or against Arizona State because they were the No. 1 program," Bill Ewing said of his decision to play for Jim Jones at UW. "I wanted to play against the best schedule and competition. And Wyoming did that."

After graduating from UW, Bill Ewing was on the fast track to a Major League career after setting organizational records in the Angels Single-A, Double-A and Triple-A affiliates. Unfortunately, a difficult recovery from arm surgery led to a career-ending injury before Ewing ever got a call up to the big club.

"I had a very enjoyable career. For me the game in the Minor Leagues was as easy as it was that day in Fort Collins," Ewing said. "I had broken every Angels record at the minor-league stops. I was never under 100 RBIs and always over 25 home runs. It looked like I was going up. You never know. All that time I had been blessed."

Al Kincaid's tenure as Wyoming football coach was as mediocre as it can get—a 29-29 record over five seasons (1981-85). But it should be noted that Kincaid recruited the most prolific home run hitter in UW history.

Sky Smeltzer began his Cowboys career as an offensive tackle but was injured during his second season at UW, forcing him to give up the gridiron and return to the sport he truly loved. First-year UW baseball coach Bill Kinneberg welcomed Smeltzer to his program in 1986 and inserted the left-handed slugger into the middle of the most statistically potent lineup in the program's history. Cowboy Field, already a difficult venue for opponents to adapt to, became a house of horrors for pitchers from the visiting bullpen.

"In high school I was a foul ball hitter," said Smeltzer, a product of Denver's Cherry Creek High School. "I led Colorado in foul ball home runs. I always had power, but our hitting coach at Wyoming (Dave Legg) straightened my swing out."

With his strength, sweet stroke and occasional help from the stiff breeze at 7,200 feet, Smeltzer belted a UW record 46 career home runs from 1986-89.

"Cowboy Field was a really big park. I believe it was 360 (feet) down the lines and 380 in the gaps," Smeltzer said. "At 7,200 feet the ball really carried. If it didn't go out, you could turn it into a lot of doubles and triples."

Smeltzer also ranks third in Cowboys history for RBIs (179) and fourth in runs scored (161). He is just ahead of former Major League standout Greg Brock (171 RBIs and 149 runs scored from 1976-79) in both categories.

The UW record book is dominated by players from Kinneberg's great teams of the late 1980s and early 1990s.

Mike Mulvaney (1985-88) is the 'Pokes record holder for RBIs (194), runs scored (193) and hits. The talented infielder is also second in career doubles (55), behind Brock (57), and third in home runs (37). Not bad for a lightly recruited player from Arvada West (CO) High School.

"I was just an above-average high school hitter with an average defensive game," Mulvaney said. "I wanted an opportunity to play, and Wyoming was one of two schools that had me on a visit. I jumped all over it. It was a great opportunity. . . .

"I was born and raised a country guy. I was all about hunting and fishing, and it was like Coach (Jim) Jones knew that. I had been up to Miracle Mile fishing with my uncle and grew up a hunter."

Jones guided UW to a disappointing 19-27 record in 1985, his 14th and final season as the head coach. However, he left the cupboard nice and full for Kinneberg. In 1986, the Cowboys won the Eastern Division of the WAC and finished 29-19 overall. UW would set a new program record for wins in 1989 (36) and again in 1990 (37).

"You look at the WAC during that time and it was usually who out-hit who. There was not a lot of pitching, and curveballs didn't break a lot in Laramie. It was when you had to go out on west coast trips where you would learn to pitch and play defense," Mulvaney said. "We did some real good things. The chemistry on those teams was outstanding. There weren't many years that weren't fun for me at Wyoming. Baseball made life fun for me."

Wyoming wasn't just producing big-time hitters during the era. Barry Goldman won a program-record 30 games from 1988-91. The right-hander from Cherry Creek High School went on to play in the Independent League and was one of the Colorado Rockies replacement players at the beginning of the 1995 season before the Major League Baseball strike ended. Scott Freeman (1988-90), who is tied for second on UW's wins list with 18, was a second-round draft pick of the Los Angeles Dodgers in 1990. Rigo Beltran, a brilliant left hander (1990-91), went on to pitch in the Major Leagues for the St. Louis Cardinals (1997), New York Mets (1998-99), Colorado Rockies (1999-2000) and Montreal Expos (2004). He is currently the pitching coach for the Cincinnati Reds Single-A team.

"You look back at it now, we had some great teams, and we were playing against great teams like Hawaii, BYU, San Diego State," Mulvaney said. "When you're a kid you don't realize the opportunities we had."

Mulvaney credits his teammates—including Ken Lake, UW's all-time leader in walks (104)—for allowing him to be the Cowboys RBIs and hits king.

"I was a doubles hitter and RBIs came natural at 7,200 feet," Mulvaney said. "You're only as good as the guys who get on in front of you."

Mulvaney proved to be a good hitter at any altitude. In 1989 with the Greensboro Hornets he broke Don Mattingly's RBI record in the Single-A franchise and was the minor league player of the year in the Cincinnati Reds organization. He climbed as high as Triple-A and even went to spring training with the Reds big league club before deciding to end his playing career.

"My wife was pregnant with our daughter back in Laramie, and I decided not to ride buses anymore," Mulvaney said.

Mulvaney returned to Arvada to begin his teaching career. For 13 years he also served as the head baseball coach at the Colorado School of Mines. When UW decided to cut the baseball program in 1996, Mulvaney felt as if he had just been plunked in the ribs with a 90 mph fastball.

"It was just kind of a lost feeling in my gut. At the time I was coaching at Mines and had called (UW) coach (David) Taylor about getting a game with them," Mulvaney said. "The next thing I know, they were losing the program. . . .

"I talked to Jeff Huson and Greg Brock, and we all said, 'What can we do?' We wrote letters and everything else but it didn't stop it. It was a bad day for baseball in this region."

Smeltzer is the head baseball coach at Yavapai (AZ) College. He was hired in 1996 and has more wins than any coach in the history of the National Junior College Athletic Association program.

"I would love nothing more than for Wyoming to bring baseball back and have somebody break my (home run) record," Smeltzer said. "I'd love to be the coach there. That would be a dream job."

The dream is over and the record books will likely remain untouched. Some other notable UW all-time career leaders include:

Batting average: 1. Mark Roberts (1989-90) .412; 2. Bill Ewing (1974-76); 3. Mulvaney .396

At-bats: 1. Charlie Angelini (1973-76) 701; 2. Ken Madia (1971-74) 683; 3. Mulvaney 659

Doubles: 1. Brock 57; 2. Mulvaney 55; 3. Bill Ewing 50

Triples: 1. Angelini 20; 2. Jerry Marion (1964-66) 18; 3. Mike Mading (1974-76) 16

Home runs: 1. Smeltzer 46; 2. Lake 38; 3. Mulvaney 37

Stolen bases: 1. Joe Ewing (1974-77) 79; 2. Ev Bufus (1966-68) 72; 3. Marion 62

Runs: 1. Mulvaney 193; 2. Lake 163; 2. Craig Maki (1985-88) 163; 4. Smeltzer 161

Hits: 1. Mulvaney 261; 2. Brock 251; 3. Maki 232

Walks: 1. Lake 104; 2. Brock 95; 3. Bob Scherger (1975-78) 94

Winning percentage: 1. Mike Shultis (1991-92) .750 (18-6); 2. Barry Goldman (1988-91) .714 (30-12)

Earned run average: 1. Bill Ewing 2.45; 2. Steve Warren (1967-69) 2.77; 3. Jim MacDonnell (1967-69) 2.82

Complete games: 1. Matt Sterling (1968-71) 23; 2. John Hilts (1965-67) 21; 2. Mike Jones (1970-73) 21; 4. Mike Larkin (1970-73) 20

Wins: Goldman 30; 2. Hilts 21; 3. Sterling 18; 3. Scott Freeman (1988-90) 18

Saves: 1. Chuck Hensala (1982-85) 13; 2. Steve Vernola (1989-90) 10; 3. Jason Kummerfeldt (1991-92) 8

Innings pitched: 1. Jones 314; 2. Larkin 295; 3. Vance Spence (1981-84) 292

Strikeouts: 1. Sterling 247; 2. Brent Foshie (1966-68) 228 (3)

Wyoming coach Bud Daniel chats with longtime rival and friend George "Stormy" Petrol, his legendary counterpart at New Mexico.

CHAPTER 12

Of the Training Room and "Two Bar"

John Omohundro, athletic trainer 1964-67

One very vivid memory I have from my time at Wyoming occurred on my first trip with the baseball team during our annual spring training excursion to the southwest and southern California colleges. We always had the very best road trips a team could ever hope for or anticipate. Our annual pilgrimage to the desert southwest always led to a lot of fun during preparation for the regular league season. While it was all serious, there were some very humorous things that would happen at the most unexpected times.

I am sure most everyone associated with the program remembers Col. Pat Murray—Bud Daniel's very good friend, actually a friend of all of us—who was a retired UW baseball booster. He would get a new Cadillac about every two years, and Daniel, Col. Murray and maybe a graduate assistant coach would lead the caravan to our various road game destinations. The next in line was another graduate assistant coach, and the third vehicle was driven by the athletic trainer. The caravan kept the players from having to drive and prevented them from getting lost along the way.

Col. Murray was initially unable to make the trip to Phoenix one year due to some health problems consisting of prolonged coughing episodes and feeling poorly for extended times. He was recovering well, but the other problem was that his new Cadillac had not yet arrived by the departure date. So the plan was that he would follow on his own and meet us at our game when he could, wherever that would be.

About the third night of our road trip we were in Arizona. I was summoned to Daniel's room and there stood Col. Murray. He had bandages all over him, bumps, bruises, cuts, lacerations and a big lesion on his scalp. I looked at him and asked, "What in the hell happened to you?"

His story was that once he had delivery of his new Cadillac he departed as soon as possible to escape the cold and wind of the high country to get to our games. He drove all day and night. About sunrise, he was driving along the interstate with his car on cruise control. He had an onset of coughing, and, during one episode, he let the car wander a little to the side of the road. He said he hit a soft spot of sand and it just jerked the wheels suddenly to the right—down the barrow pit he went, car bucking like Red Anthill coming out of chute No. 3 at the rodeo. He said the car went through some barbed wire fencing and was just going like hell, bouncing and jostling him all about the car. He couldn't get his foot or hands to deactivate the cruise control, and the damn thing just kept going wild. He couldn't stop or steer for the longest time. The car had a mind of its own.

When he finally did get out of cruise control, he was well off the road and had been roughed up pretty good. He and the car were taken into town for care, and he was released after being checked over at the local hospital. They put on a lot of dressings to cover his wounds, but the car was a big mess. Col. Murray wasn't able to utilize his car as it needed extensive repairs, so I guess he leased or rented one and made it on in. His description of the ride and the tossing and jostling about the car was absolutely hilarious. He said he had been in a lot of military vehicles off-road but never had an experience like that. Thank God he was not seriously hurt, but it did require changing a lot of dressings for him for nearly the duration of the entire trip.

I got real close to Col. Murray after that, his back and neck were stiff as boards and he required a lot of care along the way. He told a lot of very interesting stories about the military and his experiences. I enjoyed every minute of them.

Another time, we had arrived in Phoenix and were staying at the Tempe Sands Motel, just across from the old Arizona State baseball field. We stayed in a big conference room with military-style bunk beds. The graduate assistant and I were housed with the players while the remaining travel party had regular rooms. Once we got in and settled, Daniel had a meeting regarding rules and deportment requirements, and he imposed a curfew on everybody.

We had been on a pretty rugged schedule before we arrived. En route to Arizona, we traveled to Pueblo, CO and played a game. Afterward we packed up and made our way over Taos and the snowy roads of New Mexico before arriving in Albuquerque to play the Lobos in a doubleheader the next day, then a single game the following afternoon. We then drove into Phoenix from there.

We were all tired and hungry, so everyone dispersed and was eager to get some sleep. But we had two stragglers that came after curfew. The graduate assistant at that time was Bob Tedesco, who we called "Tabasco." He had to turn the stragglers into Daniel, who went ballistic. He called everyone together and laid down the law, saying that the next people to miss curfew would probably be sent home on the dog (Greyhound). He was very emphatic to say the least. He said he wanted everyone to sign out when they left and explain where they were going. He wanted everyone to keep up on their study assignments for class time being missed at school.

The next night, Daniel came in to get the report from Tabasco and the majority of the guys had signed out to go to the Library. He smiled and felt good that his message was being heeded and felt like he let the players know they needed to honor their responsibilities. I am not sure to this day if Coach knew that one of the most popular nightspots near the ASU campus was "The Library."

Nobody that I knew of would tell Daniel as he was so obviously pleased that his guys were all so dedicated. Nobody was late, but they sure had a great time going to The Library. I can't help but believe Bud knew secretly, but he never let on to me or anyone else that he may have known. It got to be comical, as nearly the entire team would sign out to The Library, so it all just added to the fun of the experience.

Another fun time was when we played ASU, which was like playing a Triple-A team in the minor leagues. They had players like Sal Bando, Sterling Slaughter, Rick Monday, the list goes on. Here we were with about three games under our belt and just a handful of outdoor practices, facing them in their 20th game.

Bobby Winkles was their manager (head coach in college terminology), and he was a legend in the ASU program. He was smart, had a great baseball mind, recruited only the best and knew how to set up an opponent. He had all of these pretty coeds as bat girls and scoreboard keepers and foul ball girls. They wore the outfits that strongly resemble the outfits you would see at Hooters nowadays. They were always there at the park to assist the visiting team with their needs prior to the game.

We went over a lot earlier than most of the team to get things in order and work with some of the players who needed treatment. We were met by one of the "hostesses," and she was a rookie in the program. She very politely introduced herself and said she would be available to help with anything we needed for our game. We asked if she could get us some towels and have someone set up some water in the dugout. She got that all taken care of and came back to ask if there was anything more. We then told her that we had noticed that the batter's box was still locked and asked if she could get us a key to unlock it. We also remarked that all of the baseballs she brought us were the same, and that we needed at least a dozen curveballs to practice with.

So off she went and about a half hour later she returned and said she asked several people for the keys to the batter's box and her request was ignored. She also said that she looked through the supply room and could not locate any curveballs and we would just have to do with what we had.

Poor girl, I wonder to this day if she ever had a clue, but she was mighty easy on the eyes. We laughed about that for the rest of the trip.

One of the most infamous stories that occurred is one I think could only happen once in 1,000 years.

We had a player named Milon "Mike" Hulbert, who was probably one of the most naturally humorous players that I ever came across. He had interesting views on life and different perspectives on things. In today's world of baseball, he would have been called flaky, but he was always "Mike being Mike." He was from Colorado and was a power-hitting first baseman. Not fast, but nifty around the bag.

Over the summer, Mike had lost his confidence with his throws back to the pitcher from first base. He could make all the other plays but for some reason he just couldn't throw accurately back to the mound after an out, around the horn or when returning the ball after a pick-off attempt. It bothered him until he worked it out in his mind that he could get it back accurately and consistently if he threw a knuckleball. Everybody would ride him unmercifully, but he had to do what he had to do.

One game, we were playing on the road, and we had the opponent down by a run in the bottom of the ninth. There were runners at first and third, and we tried the old false pickoff play of faking the throw to first and then wheeling around to catch a runner off of third. We nearly got him picked off the bag at third to end the game, but he made it back just in time. Two pitches later, it looked like we had a pickoff at first and won the game. Mike was a little upset at the missed call, and he threw the ball back to the pitcher with a little more zest, causing the pitcher to miss catching the ball by about a foot. The ball went toward the dugout, and both the catcher and third baseman went to retrieve it. The runner on third scored to tie the game, but the runner rounding second saw the shortstop was a little late in covering third so he never broke stride and continued on to third.

Once the ball was retrieved there was a futile attempt to throw to third to get the runner, and it was an errant throw to the shortstop who could not position to catch the ball and make the tag. The ball went into short left field, and the runner came home with the winning run.

I have never to this day seen a manager so angry. Bud looked like he could have a coronary at any minute, his neck and face were red and he was just beside himself. He went over to the pitcher and asked what the hell was up and that he should catch the ball. The pitcher said that Mike threw that damn knuckle-ball back with a lot of zip, and it just moved on him. With that he left the pitcher alone and went sprinting out to where Mike was standing and had a very lengthy and loud conversation with him. Some of it needed translation he was so angry.

The thing that ended up being so funny was the next week in practice; Mike tried throwing normally back to the pitcher to no avail. Coach outlawed him from throwing the knuckler, so Mike practiced all week and made all of his throws back to the pitcher without a problem. With about two games left in the season, Daniel remarked in the dugout how his talk had finally gotten through to Mike, and he was at last throwing the ball back to the pitcher accurately and consistently. He hoped it was a lesson Mike could build on in the future.

Tabasco leaned over to me in the dugout and said, "Do you think this would be a good time to tell Bud that he now throws a forkball back to the pitcher?" I just looked at him in shock and said not unless you want to see World War III break out. I am not sure if Coach ever did know the "rest of the story."

Another time, we left Arizona having played a brutal amount of games. All of the pitchers were getting early overuse soreness from throwing so much, and we were putting more and more time into treating and stretching in an effort to keep them as fresh as possible.

We were driving in the early morning hours over to San Diego, having left Tucson going through Yuma. It was a particularly boring stretch of highway, and we were all tired from the games the day before and packing up to leave. As the sun began to rise, I was becoming real drowsy so I decided to catch up to the van ahead and have a graduate assistant see if he could relieve me for a while on driving.

I pulled up next to the other van and there on top of the bags of equipment was Ken Hemming, a pitcher who was due to start later that day in San Diego, and he was totally out. He looked like a largemouth bass—mouth open so wide—I had to look twice because it was a scary sight to see, like something from a horror show. The second time I looked more closely and found it so funny to look at. Ken looked like he had been dead for several weeks with his mouth agape.

I immediately lost all my drowsiness and had a chuckle to the point I was laughing aloud. The guy riding shotgun, I believe it was Don Cadman, woke up and asked why I was laughing. I just pointed out the window. He could not let the moment be wasted and awakened the rest in the van to see the sight, which attracted more interest than seeing the Grand Canyon. When we all stopped for gas and eats, Ken was hit with some unmerciful ribbing. He went out on the mound and had a great game. That sight was uglier than sin dipped in misery.

Who could ever forget our trip to the University of Arizona in Tucson? The Wildcats manager, Frank Sancet, and the athletic department had arranged for a goodwill game to be played in the early evening. The game was well attended and we won. Afterward, both teams were taken across the border into Nogales, Mexico for a real fiesta. The place backed into a small mountain and was almost like a cave. It had *mariachi* bands, dancers and was a very festive occasion. I continue to have particularly fond memories about the place.

Earlier in the day, I had talked with Bud about potential problems we might have drinking the water in Mexico. Those were the days before bottled water. So he thought about that for a while and then gathered the team after the game. Everyone was really happy because of the win, and he said: "Men, and I mean it when I say men, this will be the first and only time I recommend you don't drink the water over there. You are allowed to drink beer."

At first they thought he was kidding, but when they realized he was not, there were a lot of happy campers going to dinner. What a great time, first time many of us had ever had a rattlesnake meat appetizer. Good thing they furnished a bus to take us back to Arizona.

Lastly, I have to confess a story I had never told Daniel before so that it can come out now in this book.

As most know, Daniel was a Colonel in the Marines. He had a lot of military friends and contacts. One such contact happened to be with the Marine Corps Recruit Depot in San Diego. He was able to arrange lodging for us during our stay in San Diego. We pulled into the base and were assigned some squad bays in the enlisted men's quarters.

Being an officer, Coach was provided with a couple of rooms in the officer's quarters. When we got settled, Bud asked me to get some provisions for him as he was going to be entertaining some of the base people for a small reception. I said I would hop right to it, got into the car and headed toward the main gate. About 100 yards from the gate, I see these dreaded police lights flashing behind me, and they waved me over. I saw this one guy who looked like he had just been to an NFL Pro Bowl. He was the biggest soldier I had ever seen, and he is all dressed in his finest spit and polish uniform, accompanied by a smaller Marine, who was the driver.

The big one came rapidly walking over. I could hear him mumbling, and when he got to me, he said, "Boy, what in the hell do you think you are doing?"

I said I was on an errand for our manager and was with the Wyoming baseball team. I asked if I had done something wrong. He just glowered a minute (seemed like an hour) and then leaned down and asked for my license, which I showed to him. He was still really angry. He handed it back to me, asked me a bunch of questions and said he was going to take me in, asking me if I knew where I was driving.

I told him I was on my way out the gate to run an errand for our coach. He said: "Stow that bullshit; you were driving on our parade ground, and nobody drives on that. Ever!"

I apologized and explained that I thought it was a big parking lot. He looked like a vein was going to pop in his neck, and he yelled: "A parking lot? Boy, that is hallowed ground. You just insulted every Marine on this base."

I sounded like a motorboat—but . . . but . . . but . . . but—and he checked the license plate. His buddy, the driver, asked who was in charge and what was I doing on this base. I told him about being with the baseball team, and we were here for a few days to play some games nearby. He asked again who was in charge. I said: "The manager is Bud Daniel, and he is a Colonel in the Marine Corps and that is how we got on the base."

They were not paying much attention until I mentioned Bud's name and his military rank. They looked at one another and asked if he had warned me not to drive on our parade ground. I said I guess he took it for granted that I knew about that, but I swear he never said a thing to me.

The driver conferred with the big guy for a minute, made a call, then came back to my car and said, "Your story matches. We have decided to let you off with a warning, but if we ever see you doing that again, you will be in big trouble. Do you hear that?"

I was shaking in my boots and saying, "yes, sir," loud and clear. You will never see me on this parade ground again ever. The big guy said he was not bluffing, and I took him at his word and slowly made my way out the gate, returned and went to my squad bay, never told anyone about that until now. That was something I have never forgotten, indelibly etched you might say.

I spent a lot of years at the University of Wyoming. There are many fond memories from those days. I lived a lifetime of fun, enjoyment, excitement, satisfaction and received a wonderful education to prepare me for my future. I feel extremely fortunate to have met and associated with such wonderful people such as Coach Daniel and the players.

The baseball program held particularly fond memories and enjoyment for me. My background was in minor league baseball prior to my enrolling at the University, and I always looked at it as an extension of that while with the baseball program. Bud always treated me so very well, with kindness, dignity and respect. I always feel honored to have been a part of his program.

(*Author's note:* Omohundro graduated from UW with a Bachelor's Degree in Education and went on to get a Master's Degree in Physical Therapy. He became the head trainer for the Cardinals NFL franchise when it was located in St. Louis and remained with the team after the move to Arizona. He was inducted into the Missouri Athletic Hall of Fame. Omohundro retired in 2008 after spending 41 years with the Cardinals.)

Jack Allen, football player/baseball fan
1952, 1955-59

As is so typical of many high school students, I wasn't sure what I was going to do after graduation. A football scholarship from the University of Wyoming set the course for me in the fall of 1952. I roomed at the athletic dorm and had a quick introduction to college and dormitory life. As a freshman, I learned to walk softly among the upper classmen as there was a definite hierarchy. Freshmen were segregated and roomed on the third floor. It was fortunate other athletes from my high school were in the dorm to help my comfort level. Food at the training table prepared by Willie and

Daphne wasn't like Mom's, but it kept us bulky! Freshmen washed pots and pans and cleaned the Fieldhouse after games for $15 a month.

Coach Bowden Wyatt was an All-American football player from Tennessee. At practice one day, a tailback by the name of Spaulding was running a play. Wyatt was not satisfied and told him to run it again. He had him run it for the third time after which, in exasperation, he told Spaulding: "Get out of there! You can't make the length of your nose!" Joe Mastrogiovanni, our quarterback, who had an extremely large nose, said, "If that was me I could have made ten yards."

After my freshman year, I left school, enlisted in the Army and spent over two years in Korea, returning in October of 1955. Phil Dickens was now the UW football coach. After one year as a redshirt, I was again a member of the team that went 10-0 and declined an invitation to the Sun Bowl, holding out for a better invite that never came. After Dickens departed for Indiana, Bob Devaney took over and was extremely successful. Again in 1959, Wyoming was invited to the Sun Bowl.

I had the unusual fortune to play for three of the most successful football coaches in the history of Wyoming. The camaraderie, which was such a major part of living and playing with fellow athletes in all sports, has resulted in lifetime friendships. Many of the football players had the opportunity to play baseball as well. Those of us who did not formed the cheering section at the games. The many reunions held in Lander are most significant. The athletes in all sports who lived in the athletic dormitory attend and participate in golf outings, picnics and wonderful evening celebrations.

The University of Wyoming shaped my life in nothing but positive ways.

The world's greatest "pepper" game, 1959.
From left: Joe Netherton, Col. Murray, and Jim Walden.

Coach Daniel at the
Detroit Tiger's Spring
Training camp, 1959,
with his host,
Yankee Hall of Famer
Joe "Flash" Gordon.

Carl Splitt, football player 1957-59

Gene Domzalski, an eight-year veteran of the New York Yankees organization, was an All-Conference infielder at Wyoming and was also an all-conference halfback on the football team. He was the only sophomore football player Bob Devaney ever released from spring football drills. Domzalski had signed a bonus contract with the Yankees after one baseball season. I host a Cowboy golfing group in Tucson at a desert course covered with many types of large cacti ringing each fairway. I reminded each player that if they accidentally stray one of their massive drives into the cactus patch not to go after the wayward balls. It's not worth running into the painful needles of the cactus or a diamondback snake. On the second hole of one match, our strong Domzalski ignored the warning and went to retrieve his ball saying, "Oh heck, I'll be OK." But after a 15-second walk in the desert he came out with cactus spikes on his arms, legs and hands. He had blood oozing out of the wounds, and, in his Polish/Pennsylvanian accent he uttered, "Boy, those Chaloopas really got me!"

Bruce Haroldson, coach, Ft. Lewis 1961-62

After locating the site of the first baseball meeting scheduled for the Ft. Lewis Rangers, I looked around for the man in charge, but I could not for the life of me see anyone who looked distinguished enough to validate my inspection. Then from the corner of my eye I spotted a glare off of two bars of silver and, alas, my first meeting with Bud Daniel (alias "Two Bar" to any player remotely connected to the Ft. Lewis baseball program).

The Rangers were also known as a bunch of pissed off pros who, instead of throwing strikes, missing curveballs and getting paid for it, were now "ground pounders" and jeep drivers, courtesy of the Berlin crisis. After my initial tryout, I found my niche as a mop-up pitcher with some duty as game time and dugout entertainer. Some of my off duty time was spent at times wrestling with telephone booths. With this invaluable experience gained under the tutelage and complete endorsement from Two Bar, and after receiving my discharge, I could hardly wait to embrace the guidance once more from my mentor.

This came soon enough when I was invited to chaperone Daniel for the University of Wyoming's trip to the College World Series. Since Coach was now the President of the ABCA, I was in for a week in the fast lane. Never had I seen so many kiss ups to the world's tallest midget. Boy, did we have it made. First class suite, free booze, two sandbagger golfing coaches who ripped off all my spending money for the trip. And we found time for some wonderful days and nights of college baseball.

Now I couldn't just call it quits as a hero worshiper of the now illustrious Two Bar. I just had to reconnect with the traveling Cowboys on their annual trip to Arizona and Las Vegas. It was here that I saw a weakness in the coaching style and techniques used by Two Bar that he had forgotten to implement from the knowledge gained at Ft. Lewis. He needed someone to shake up the sunburned Cowboys. So after an invite to follow the team to Vegas and hold Daniel's resin bag for him, I sensed an opportunity to bring my dugout entertainment skills as a gift to the Cowboy Joes. When all looked bleak and Coach had lost his quick step to the third base coaching box and back, I decided to loosen them up a little and proceeded to take the bag of baseballs and scattered them wildly out in front of the dugout. There were balls everywhere, and the players were looking at me like I was from a different planet.

Two Bar was cracking up because he knew where I was coming from. The Cowboys started a rally, won the game and then we all went out and tried to find some girls. I should have brought the bag of balls.

Gary Cowan, Wyoming assistant coach 1965-69

My involvement with Wyoming baseball really started on the west coast. I played for Bud Daniel at Ft. Lewis, WA as a result of being recalled during the Cuban Missile Crisis. Since he was a Captain in the Wyoming National Guard and was also recalled, he went by the nickname of "Two Bar" with the members of the ball club.

After we were released from active duty and I finished my undergraduate degree at Brigham Young University, I called Daniel and advised him I wanted to attend law school at Wyoming and asked if he needed an assistant coach. He arranged for an interview with the Dean of the College of Law and offered me a job. I arrived in Laramie for the spring semester in 1965 during the late evening in the middle of a ferocious windstorm. The plan was to live with Bud and his three young sons in married student housing. I had just traded for an older Porsche vehicle before heading to Laramie and did not realize that it had a considerable degree of rust throughout. As I pulled into the parking lot of the housing complex and opened the door to get out, a huge gust of wind ripped the door off its hinges. So there I was standing in the middle of the parking lot looking down at the driver's side door to my car as it hit the ground. Welcome to Laramie!

Coaching baseball on the High Plains was certainly a challenge that the other schools in the Conference did not share. When the team would return from the spring training trip to Arizona in high spirits there would be, in all likelihood, several inches of snow on the field and then it was back in the Fieldhouse for practice. Team morale would plummet, and we would have to get the team charged up in preparation for a trip to Salt Lake City, where we would be playing six games in five days against Utah. On road trips, one of my main duties was bed check as there was always a team curfew. There are several college graduates out there, who will remain anonymous, who owe their college degrees to my discretion in not reporting curfew violations. The spring training trip was usually to Tempe, the home of Arizona State University. Their coach would make arrangements for us to stay at the Sands Motel across the street from the campus.

One memorable day, I was playing an early morning round of golf with Bud's son, Tim, at Papago Municipal. The team was to leave for a game across town at Grand Canyon College at 11 a.m. Tim and I were late, so the team left without us. I had to hire a cab to get us to the field in time for the game. Needless to say, Bud was pretty furious at both of us. I was lucky he didn't send me back to Laramie, as he had not hesitated to do that very thing to another assistant who broke the rules.

Thanks to Bud's patience and encouragement, I was able to graduate from the law school in the spring of 1969 and have now been a practicing trial lawyer in Colorado for over 40 years.

Tim Daniel, son of UW Coach Bud Daniel

Q: *Who can ruin baseballs faster than mosquitoes swarm in Wyoming?*

A: *The Daniel Boys.*

Growing up, my brothers (Tom and Mark) and I would take a brand new, shiny white baseball out of its box and go outside and find ways to nick, cut, rip, wet and muddy it in an instant. The three of us managed to ensure that no one associated with Cowboys baseball went untouched. We weren't brats. Well, I certainly wasn't, not so sure about the other two knuckleheads. We were energetic, curious and unrelentingly demanding of our share of attention. So it is safe to say we were serious pests.

Each of the boys appreciated how lucky we were to have our father and to be growing up so closely associated with baseball. How many other kids in town were able to meet famous ballplayers? How many other kids could say that a Hall of Fame pitcher, in this case Lefty Gomez of the New York Yankees, came to stay with them? Yep, he called my brother Tom and me both "Charley" because he could never figure out the names and the faces. He became the officially funniest man I would ever meet. He was a great ballplayer but I got the sense he was a great man, too. The added dividend was that he was a serious hoot. You could listen to him spin stories and laugh continuously night and day. When you heard a story about the Babe Ruth or Lou Gehrig, you knew that you were blessed to be around someone who was very special. Our father was special, too, because don't believe for a moment that he couldn't hold court with the best of them. We were lucky, very lucky.

In the decades of the 1950s and 1960s, we had a chance to be around and play with all of the interesting characters that made up Wyoming baseball during those years. The opportunities our father presented us were important, even though we didn't know exactly how important at the time. The players' laughter and their pranks, their victories and how they lost with a "we'll get them next time" attitude, was special for the Daniel boys.

In Wyoming you don't just go outside and play ball. It is rarely that easy. You have to get psyched up to go out into the elements and play ball and that always took a few minutes of thinking about how much you really wanted to play in a 30 mph wind or the cold. And one those rare warm summer nights you also had to share the field (and give some blood to) with swarms of hungry mosquitoes.

You have to really want to play ball if you come to Wyoming. So the young men who showed up to play didn't approach life in measured tones. Each player in his unique way became an important piece of my life and memories. Yeah, it was a great time.

(*Author's note:* Tim Daniel earned a Bachelor's Degree at UW in 1975 and an Master's Degree from Webster University in 1982. He enlisted in the US Army Corps of Engineers and retired after 28 years of active duty and was inducted into the University of Wyoming Army ROTC Hall of Fame).

Bud Daniel holds the Skyline Conference championship trophy while reaching out for the District VII championship trophy after Wyoming clinched a berth in the 1956 College World Series. Pat Sturnian, a Coca-Cola distributor, makes the presentation.

CHAPTER 13

Cowboys Forever!

Through these halls have walked great men
They served this university as students and athletes
Their performance made them honorable citizens
They established a life-long bond and a lasting legacy
Their friendships will stand the test of time
Cowboys forever!

After coaching baseball at Wyoming for 20 years (1951-71), Glenn "Bud" Daniel decided to make a permanent southern swing. Why did Daniel decide to ride off into the sunset and take a job at Arizona? The legendary Cowboy explains the decision in his own words:

There were many reasons in my thought process for leaving. Always in the back of my mind was the realization that such a large part of my life was connected to Wyoming, and I had huge appreciation for all of the opportunities, rewards, honors, and national recognition I had received while serving the University. However, the world of college baseball had gone through many changes. The attitudes, responsibilities, lifestyles and coaching camaraderie were changing in many different directions.

I had for the last five or more years had a desire to get into the administrative end of athletics. I also realized that coaching had become a younger man's challenge. Not only had recruiting, travel and finances all changed, but also the attitudes of prospective recruits. The young men of the 1970s had great expectations in the way of financial aid. "What can you give me?" became the attitude instead of "What are my opportunities?"

During my entire career at Wyoming I was able to have a great deal of freedom in what I could offer a recruit in the way of aid. It ranged from full scholarship, including board, room, tuition and books, to any combination. I could foresee what the NCAA would do in the near future as to the number of scholarships and all forms of aid. NCAA oversight of shorter schedules and the number of players a coach could have on the team were all on the horizon. Many of these changes were brought about by the ridiculous interpretation of Title IX by the Secretary of Education's office. I do not know any head coaches that are not in favor of improving programs for the female athletes. But it meant the doom of many male programs. Wyoming did not have to give in to the demands of Title IX.

When I reviewed the sport information and my own records of the years that Wyoming went to Arizona and California on the spring baseball trips, my reactions were varied. I was amazed and flattered by what my guys accomplished. We played the very best teams in the country. We did not win as many as we would have liked, but by the time we returned to Wyoming we were a vastly improved team. When I was hired by Red Jacoby, he insisted that I take part in the then American Association of College Baseball Coaches. Through the AACB, I made contacts and befriended the many coaches who would schedule us on their spring trips. It took a lot of imagination and work to put together the great band of Wyoming boosters who each year would furnish their cars and drive the many miles our schedules demanded. They joined us in living in stadium dressing rooms, eating in university dining facilities, playing early morning golf games, and rooting for the team in the doubleheaders we often played. We really became a "Band of Brothers" each spring.

As I look back, I realize that the change in travel restrictions, legal modifications and many other NCAA policies would have prevented the spring trips and the opportunity for the Cowboys to play the best baseball schedule a coach could arrange. When I received the opportunity in 1971 to accept a position in the Athletic Department at the University of Arizona, I never imagined that baseball at Wyoming would ever be dropped in favor of a couple of women's sports programs. Frankly, in my opinion, it was a gigantic bureaucratic political mistake. One of the reasons given was to save $200,000. This should have been an embarrassment to the UW administration.

The AACBC, now called the American Baseball College Association, would become a large part of my baseball activities. The more I participated in their programs, the larger my responsibilities grew. I was honored to be elected their national president in 1963. I was elected chairman of the ABCA Board of Directors for 1993-95 and still serve on the board. My membership is approaching 60 years, and I am the only living past president to have personally associated with every president in the history of the ABCA. This is a fact that I am extremely proud to claim.

I'd like to mention some of the great Wyoming Cowboys who have passed away over the years . . .

Don Napierkowski, outfield, 1952-56)

Don was the ideal athlete, a good student and a great competitor. He was well-liked by the entire student body, respected by his teammates, always a gentleman. After graduating from Wyoming with a degree in Business in 1956, the two-time All-American was signed by the Cincinnati Reds organization. After graduation he was commissioned a 2ND Lieutenant in the USAF and entered pilot training, eventually stationed at Davis-Monthan AFB Base, Tucson, AZ. Don suffered fatal injuries in an automobile crash near Yuma, AZ, in 1959, leaving the world far too soon. He was inducted posthumously into the Wyoming Athletic Hall of Fame in 2006.

Bill Meeboer, pitcher, 1953-56

Bill was a Laramie High School graduate, who had only played American Legion baseball sparingly before arriving on the UW campus. He worked hard and earned a spot in the rotation for the Cowboys in his junior and senior years, developing into an important part of the 1956 CWS team. He graduated with a degree in Business and attended a baseball reunion in 2003 before passing away soon after. He also was inducted into the UW athletic hall of fame posthumously in 2006, along with the CWS squad.

Dennis Seiler, outfield, 1959) and
Tommy Thomas, outfield, 1956-58

Dennis and Tommy died tragically together from asphyxiation in their Laramie apartment in November of 1959, due to a faulty gas heater. They had planned to move into the Athletic Dorm the next weekend. Their deaths took an emotional toll on the UW baseball family. Both young men were from Montana and laid to rest in Billings.

John Hilts, pitcher, 1964-67

John was one of the most successful pitchers in UW history and spent time in the Baltimore Orioles organization before coaching the Medford American

Legion program to an Oregon state title in 1976. John, who went on to be a successful attorney, passed away in 2006 at the age of 61 after a five-year battle with cancer.

Nick Popravak, second base, 1953

Nick was one of the first recruits from Chicago's Bowen High School. He played one year with the Cowboys before signing a professional contract in the St. Louis Cardinals organization. An automobile accident cut his life short.

Bob Villasenor, pitcher, 1953-56

Bob was a vital part of the three Skyline Championships, winning one game in each of those playoffs. He was an All-Conference selection in 1956 and was the winning pitcher for UW in the CWS victory over New York University. When our 1956 team was nominated for induction into Wyoming's Athletic Hall of Fame in 2006, I phoned Bob, and he was thrilled to receive the news. Sadly, Bob's second battle with leukemia prevented him from joining his teammates in Laramie. His sons, Mike and Bill, were able to attend and filmed the induction, which Bob was able to see before he passed away.

Dick Olejnik, infield, 1952-54

Dick came to UW with the group from Chicago's Bowen High School. He played on the first Skyline Championship team at third base. He earned a degree in business and passed away in 1994.

Coach Ev Shelton

From left: Don Napierkowski, Vince Zimmer, and Ed Litecky

Vince Zimmer, utility, 1962-63

Vince was a center on Bob Devaney's football team. Just prior to Wyoming's November game with Arizona he was notified to report for active duty with the Wyoming Army National Guard. His request for a student deferment was denied, and he joined me on active duty for the Cuban Missile Crisis. At the Ft. Lewis Army Base in Tacoma, WA, he played baseball while stationed there. Vince's contributions to the Lander reunions and the outstanding organization he helped to create will live on for a very long time. There is no university of college that we know of in the country that can in any way duplicate the *esprit de corps* exhibited by over 100 Wyoming athletes every three years at the Lander gatherings. They look forward to and cherish each event. Vince passed away in 2005 from leukemia.

Ed Litecky, infield, outfield, pitcher, 1951-55

Ed's widow, Maxine, described him as shy and home-sick for Chicago until settling into and falling in love with Wyoming. After Ed got out of the Army, the couple drove their green Plymouth station wagon, which they bought from me, back to Wyoming to see the mountains. Maxine also remembers former Yankees second baseman, Joe Gordon, scouting the Cowboys for the Detroit Tigers and telling her that Ed was too slow for the big leagues. When Ed died, legendary sports writer Larry Birleffi wrote the following about him:

> *"My own Rogers Hornsby." That is what I always called Ed Litecky when he was hitting around .400 on the Wyoming baseball team. Ed came out from eastern tough country for a while to play baseball and to go to school at Laramie. He stayed for a lifetime, spreading a contagious smile through the years. In baseball he could have played in the big leagues. In golf he carried*

the same swing and hit long irons as effective as anybody I've seen. Ed will be missed, and so will his unique parlay games in the fall that were patently his and a lot of fun to play. He left this earth far too soon! Nine members of Wyoming's defending loop champions were give honors on the Skyline all Eastern division baseball teams as picked by coaches of the schools on this side of the Rockies. Yet there was one name that was conspicuous in its absence from the first team roster, the name would be undoubtedly the most versatile player in either division, Ed Litecky. A sophomore, the genial "Chicagoan" second sacker was also called upon to pitch, play third and the outfield. A consistent .290 hitter, but the real payoff over his career was the ability to come up with a game winning hit, his ability to come through with a clutch hit or home run.

Matt Sterling, pitcher, 1968-71

Matt was recruited with Bill Stearns and Syd Taylor out of Denver in 1968. His junior year he led the Cowboys with a 7-3 record and an earned-run average of 3.19. I remember a game at the Colorado School of Mines when the very supportive fathers of Matt and Bill arrived at the baseball field in a limousine. When they opened the door, Matt and Bill stepped out on the red carpet, the crowd roared and the Cowboys won! Matt died tragically in Denver after graduating from UW.

Rick O'Daniels, infield, 1969-72

Rick was a left-hander from Burlington, Iowa, who we moved to first base. He was an All-WAC selection in 1971 and 1972. I used to tell the players to take diligent care of their Louisville Slugger bats and even take them to bed if necessary. Rick and his new bride were invited to my house for supper one evening and she said: "Coach, does Rick really have to take his new Louisville Slugger to bed with him each night?" Rick passed away in 2009.

Vic McElroy, utility, 1954-56

Vic was a fine utility player and a fiery competitor on the Skyline Championship teams of 1955-56 and played in the CWS. He was posthumously inducted into the Wyoming Athletic Hall of Fame Class of 2006. He coached and taught in the Bakersfield, CA, school system before passing away in 2003.

Gerry Nagle, infield, 1952-56

Gerry came to Laramie all the way from Lynn, MA and naturally became friends with Frank Goodie, who had grown up in Portland, ME. After graduation, Gerry taught school in Cheyenne, in California and eventually in Scottsdale, AZ, where he was a leader in the National Education Association before passing away in 1979 at the age of 49. He was a solid player who was inducted posthumously into the Wyoming Athletic Hall of Fame in 2006.

Dave Brickley, pitcher, 1967-70

Dave was an outstanding pitcher and one of the lucky group who participated in the Riverside (CA) Invitational and the Air Force Invitational in Hawaii, plus the three-game series against Arizona and Arizona State. His daughter told me that Dave, who died in 2009, often talked of that experience.

Joe Netherton, outfield, 1958-61

Joe was a good hitter and serious competitor, who was also friends with many of UW's wrestlers and football players as he had a passion for their sports as well. After graduation he returned to Missouri where he expanded the family cattle farm. He battled Lou Gehrig's disease valiantly before passing away in 2009. His wife, Phyllis, took over the business since his passing.

Mike Rawson, infield, 1962-63

Mike played for the Cowboys when I was away on active duty. In 1963 he led the team in hitting (.432) and hit seven home runs. Mike died of a heart attack while seated on his tractor on the family farm in Iowa.

Tom Bournellis, infield, 1949-52

Tom played for the Cowboys after World War II alongside Gus Angelos. They were real father figures to the young Chicago boys who arrived in 1952. Tom graduated with a degree in Pharmacy and was very successful with his outlets in the San Francisco area. He even helped me recruit some players out to Wyoming over the years.

Let me draw this stroll through memory lane to a close with personal reflections and a list of some outstanding honors and thrills. I cannot mention them in order of importance because they were all special. To reflect on all of the outstanding coaches and players without omitting some would be impossible, but I will make an attempt.

Two Wyoming coaches top the list—Ev Shelton and Bill Strannigan, top the list. Ev was my coach and mentor. Bill was one of my travel partners and favorite coaches. Both are in my treasured memories. Ev was my baseball coach for two years at Wyoming. In his early sixties he would catch batting practice every day. He became a second father to me.

George Petrol (New Mexico) and Pete Butler (Northern Colorado), two great coaches, were always friendly challenges. Glen Tuckett, the BYU coach and athletic director, was always a tremendous model of integrity and leadership. A leader of leaders. In my early years, Tuckett was a serious, tough competitor on the diamond. Arizona's "Pop" McKale nominated me for the ABCA vice president chair. Three years later, I had the wonderful year as the ABCA President. Dutch Fehring (Stanford), Rod Dedeaux (USC) and Art Reichle (UCLA) were all legends in the game and dear friends. These southern California coaches were responsible for nominating me to the ABCA Hall of Fame. Rod was voted Coach of the Decade by the NCAA College World Series. Dutch was a pillar in USA Baseball and the Olympics. Art coached for years at UCLA and had a dude ranch up in the Snowy Range west of Laramie. These three will have baseball corralled for St. Peter and players ready to play in the leagues in my heaven.

Minnesota's Dick Siebert was my Hawaii-Japan clinic trip partner. Dick played in the Major Leagues with Philadelphia. He had a great sense of humor. The Japanese love movie stars and baseball players. At the bar he was Babe Ruth, and I was Mickey Rooney. All I heard was "Rooney-san—you sing, you dance?"

One of my fondest memories is of Bobby Winkles, the coaching legend at Arizona State, sitting on a tractor, dragging the infield on a Sunday morning so the Cowboys could play Michigan. He was a coach who would go all out for his opponents. He was a leader in teaching young players to hustle and have respect for the game. He later managed the Los Angeles Angels.

ABCA Board of Directors Committee partners and advisors include: Dave Keiltz, Bobo Brayton, "Tinker" Connelly, Tom Petroff and Jack Kaiser, problem solvers through thick and thin.

I had the opportunity to know and work with many professional players. What college coach ever had a Hall of Fame pitcher caddy for him on the golf course? Yankees great "Lefty" Gomez did just that for me in Laramie. His son played freshman ball for the Cowboys. My wife, Connie, wearing Yankees pinstripes, has a favorite photo with Lefty.

One of my favorite stories with Lefty was at the 1974 ABCA Convention at the Fairmont Hotel in San Francisco. Women just had been invited to the banquets for the first time. Bob Uker, the former Major League catcher, was the speaker at the noon banquet. He had, unfortunately, used some risqué language and had embarrassed several of the women in attendance. Later that day, Connie and I were standing in the lobby when Lefty and Bobby Winkles invited her to join them at the bar. I was strongly told to stay put. That evening at the Hall of Fame dinner, Winkles was the emcee and Lefty was the main speaker. The first thing Winkles said as he started the banquet: "Would Connie Daniel please stand up!" His next statement was "Lefty and I have told Mrs. Daniel every joke or story that we were going to use tonight. So you ladies can now relax." Connie could not eat a bite of dinner.

My last Lefty Gomez story takes place at the NCAA baseball Regional in Laramie. We were entering the stadium when a hitter came up with a double. Lefty says to me, "I got a double once in Yankee Stadium. I was standing by second base when the umpire hollered, 'You're out!' As I went back to the dugout I knew manager Joe McCarthy was going to be furious. I was hiding behind the water cooler when I heard him scream 'Gomez, what the hell happened at second base?' My only answer was—'How the hell do I know? It is the first time I've ever been there.'"

Joe Gordon, a Yankee Hall of Famer, spent a spring with us scouting Bob Jingling. He later was my host in "Tiger Town" at spring training in Florida. Joe and I also spent a lot of time on the golf course when our paths crossed. He could hit a golf ball out of sight. We flew his airplane to his ranch north of Sacramento where I taught Joe a simulated "carrier approach" to the landing strip. Joe uttered, "Amen." Yankees manager, Joe McCarthy, paid Joe the ultimate compliment when he said, "Joe Gordon is the best player I've ever seen."

Tommy Lasorda, the great Los Angeles Dodgers manager, joined Connie and I at several ABCA banquets, sitting at our table sharing his baseball adventures, his friendship with Frank Sinatra and a lively discussion about the best macaroni from Italy.

The honor was mine of introducing Ted Williams at a Chicago ABCA convention for his first speaking engagement. He was more nervous than I was. With a bat in hand, he did not want to stop speaking.

In the early 1970s it was breakfast with Deron Johnson and "Catfish" Hunter, riding with them to Yankee Stadium for the "old timers" game, then spending time in the Yankees dugout with a former player of mine at Ft. Lewis, Tony Kubek, a former Yankees infielder.

I also had the opportunity to meet and chat with "Sparky" Anderson, the well-known manager of the Cincinnati Reds and Detroit Tigers, when he accepted an award for his contributions to baseball at an ABCA honors luncheon.

Two men came into our lives during my recall to active duty that would become important friends, associates and members of our family, Gary Cowan and Bruce Haroldson. Gary, my assistant baseball coach for four years, completed law school and moved on to a successful legal career. Mary Francis, his wife, a successful commercial real estate broker, is an angel in our lives and companion to my wife. Bruce Haroldson and his wife, Joan, continue to be active in our lives since retirement moved them closer to us in Arizona. Basketball and baseball remain the major part of Bruce's daily schedule.

The 21 years I was associated with the University of Wyoming Athletic Department were the most satisfying years of my baseball experience. The rewards that I received financially were not that great. My largest salary was in the area of $8,500 a year. That was unreal when I look at it today. We worked very hard to realize the amount of travel our teams accomplished under a limited budget. The 1967 season travel to California, Hawaii, Utah, Arizona, New Mexico and Colorado was accomplished with $5,000. It took a lot of imagination, cooperation and desire.

My coaching record at Wyoming was 312-338 (.495), playing two-thirds of the schedule away from home, a tribute to our teams.

The athletic dorm was a major contributing factor to the success of the athletic program at UW. I was very much interested in the building as I lived there every day that I attended the University. In 1941, it was the men's residence hall, and I paid the exorbitant fee of $3 a week for my room. After returning from WWII, I returned to my dorm and lived there until I graduated in 1948. Baseball scholarship athletes were first assigned residence there in the fall of 1951. The first group were the recruits from Bowen High School in south Chicago. As freshmen, they readily accepted that for the first year, and they were required to work in the kitchen under Willie and Daphne. They ran the kitchen in a wonderful and unique way, to say the least. The early group set a standard of behavior for the baseball teams at Wyoming through 1971. The fact that the players from each sport were intermingled helped develop the wonderful spirit that exists today. They cheered each other on then and are a true support system to one another now.

I associate with many coaches from all NCAA divisions, and they continue to be amazed when I tell them of the athletic dorm and our reunions in Lander. They all wish their former athletes would remain so close and gather together similarly.

The number of young men that went through our program is unbelievable, and I'm proud to say that 98 percent of them graduated and moved on to successful and meaningful lives. They became professionals in education, business, medicine, the military, dentistry, engineering, and, yes, even in baseball and coaching. Many of these men return every few years to reunions of various types. The Lander reunions celebrate the camaraderie and *esprit de corps* of the athletes that lived in the athletic dorm. At golf outings with the teams of the mid 1950s and early 1960s our stories grow bigger and wilder, and the warmth of the memories brings us closer.

The recruiting trip of 1951 was a fascinating experience. It was my first trip into the big city, not knowing if my plans were feasible or not. Riding the elevated trains into the suburbs of south Chicago was intimidating, to say the least. The neighborhoods, in some cases, were not hospitable. When I arrived at 9600 M Street, the home of Steve Knezivich, their Polish hospitality emerged and was great. What a magic and memorable mother Mrs. Knezevich turned out to be. I felt that my recruiting evaluations would be successful, and they were. I learned how to evaluate players' athletic ability, their desire for education and the ability to get along with and to support team members.

The Hall of Fame honors started in 1984 with my induction into the Wyoming Coaches Association Hall of

Fame. In 1993, my ABCA Hall of Fame induction was at the national convention held in Atlanta. This award represented the nearly 6,000 ABCA coaching members across the nation. The association was first formed in 1945 and, up to 1993, they had awarded this honor to approximately 200 coaches. So this indeed was quite an honor from my coaching peers. I am one of the few coaches to have received the Association's Meritorious Service Award as well. Almost all of my relatives attended the banquet and, of course, I forgot to introduce my wife, Connie. My son, Tim, arrived in Atlanta with his Army Colonel's dress blue uniform ready for the occasion. Paul Roach, Wyoming's Athletic Director, flew in for the presentation. And Bob Jingling represented my ballplayers.

The University of Wyoming Athletic Hall of Fame inducted me into their 1996 class. I joined Charles "Tub" Bradley, Michelle Hoppe, Mark Miller, Jim Kiick, Larry Birleffi (my sportswriter buddy from Cheyenne) and my dear friend and longtime supporter, Senator Milward Simpson (posthumously). Each time we won a championship, the then-Governor Simpson wrote my players a letter of congratulations. His sons, Senator Al Simpson and Pete Simpson were the emcees of the event. I thanked the memories of Duke Humphrey, Red Jacoby and the Fieldhouse crew, Bob and George Prahl (Mr. Inside and Mr. Outside), for their help and work. And also LeRoy "Gabe" Gabriel for his hours making certain our field was ready for play.

Needless to say, this occasion was very emotional for me. The some 500 Cowboys fans in attendance included many of my closet friends and supporters. My fellow National Guardsmen were there as well as Connie, Tim, my three grandsons, Brad, Tommy and Tyler, and my former Assistant Coach, Gary Cowan, and his wife, Mary Frances. This banquet was shortly after Wyoming had announced the cancellation of the baseball program. I had trouble holding back my real feelings and comments. I did voice my strong opinions to merit a standing ovation from the crowd, which made me feel a little better.

The Wyoming Hall of Fame Class of 1998 included Jingling. I was very proud to see his achievements recognized.

In the spring of 2006, I learned that my team of 1956 was in contention to be inducted into Wyoming's Athletic Hall of Fame. What a momentous 50th anniversary celebration that would be of the Wyoming baseball team's participation in the CWS in Omaha. One of my former pitchers, Herb Manig, now resided in Laramie with his wife, Connie. Jim Hoppe and wife, Roberta, really got the plans going in case it would happen. We all decided to plan for a reunion that we would remember forever. When it was announced that the 1956 Cowboys were to be inductees in the 2006 Class the wires and phones got hot.

We were able to get in touch with all but one of the athletes who made the trip to Omaha. Bob Fisher could not be located. Don Napierkowski, Gerry Nagle, Vic McElhany, and Bill Meeboer had passed away. Bob Villasenor was battling cancer but vowed he would make the trip. The rest of the squad would be in attendance. Our trainer, Courtney Skinner, who had been with the three Skyline Conference Championship teams, and his family rounded out the group. Manig had been a valuable member of the 1954 and 1955 champions, but missed 1956 due to a tour in the U.S. Navy. Connie and I decided that an opening reception cocktail and dinner party would be a must.

Manig suggested that we consider renting space for those who would attend at the V-Bar Ranch resort, 20 miles west of Laramie at the base of Snowy Range. This turned out to be the best decision we could have possibly made. It was owned by the former Cowboys football player, Jim "Lefty" Cole. He and his family proved to be the perfect hosts for the event.

Invitations were mailed announcing our plans. The V-Bar offered cottages with porches overlooking the rippling waters of the Little Laramie River. We would have our breakfast, lunch and dinners as needed with full use of the John Wayne Saloon whenever we wanted. Tragedy struck when Bob Villasenor called from his deathbed and announced he could not attend. His two sons represented him at our entire affair and filmed it for Bob. Three years later we found Fisher and were able to have his plaque presented.

The players and families started arriving on Wednesday afternoon. The saloon promptly was a buzz of activity. The evening meal was scheduled at a fine cowboy steakhouse near the foot of Snowy Range. Senator Al Simpson and wife, Ann, flew in from Boston for the festivities. He made it a point to speak personally to each player and family there. At the reception I was able to express my personal reflections to all the players. It was a wonderful opportunity to express my admiration and friendship to each guy and thank them for making this event possible.

On Friday evening, before a packed house, the 1956 team was the last inductee group on the program. Fritz Heiss accepted the honors for the team and did a wonderful job. His Air Force leadership came into play. The reception and honor shown to the team was the climax of the evening. Standing ovations were the call of the night. I told the team before leaving for Omaha that the CWS would be an event they would remember forever. The fact that it was also the 50th anniversary of the trip to Omaha added to the joy of the event.

After the banquet we all returned to the V-Bar and celebrated more as if we did not want the evening to end. Sunday morning, the breakfast gathering was again an emotional and loving "good-bye" that I'm sure we will remember forever. I know that it is the reason the 1956 group is still having reunions at least every two years.

For 21 years I brought together young men in groups from Illinois, Wisconsin, California, Pennsylvania, Washington, Montana, Oklahoma, Missouri, Massachusetts, Arizona, Nebraska, Texas, Iowa, Indiana, Mississippi, Nevada, Oregon, Georgia, Washington, North Dakota, South Dakota, Minnesota, Ohio, New Jersey, Kansas and even Wyoming. I might have missed a state but we covered the nation.

With a tear in my eye and a lump in my throat I say, what a wonderful bunch of young men . . . Wyoming Cowboys all the way!

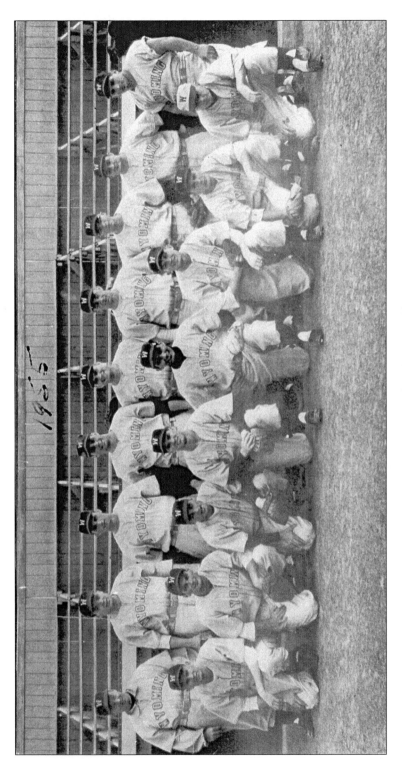

The 1955 Wyoming baseball team

CHAPTER 14

End of the Road

On January 26, 1996, the Board of Trustees—facing a projected $9.7 million budget shortfall—voted to drop baseball at the University of Wyoming. The Athletics Department was asked to cull approximately $200,000 from its books. (1)

Before he retired as Athletic Director in October 1995, Paul Roach, the beloved former Wyoming football coach, recommended the University drop men's track and field—not baseball—to save the necessary funds.

"We did a survey of alumni and some fans—a pretty good cross section of the state—and baseball was a pretty high priority to them," Roach said. "It was something they wanted."

The UW Board of Trustees rejected the notion of purging track and field and, instead, targeted baseball as part of the $6 million in cuts. Hank True was the only trustee to vote against the proposal.

"Track was something that took place in every high school," then-UW President Terry P. Roark explained. "There are (no) high school baseball teams. It probably makes more sense to keep track and field because of that. It's also a sport in which both men and women can compete."

"Did it hurt like hell to get rid of baseball? Yes, it did," said Dave Bonner, a trustee at the time. ". . . it hurt me, it pained me to be on the side that baseball should go. Baseball had to go because we had to make the budget work. At the time, we felt that was a decision that should be made and had to be made."

"It had to happen."

Baseball proponents also are still upset the trustees axed the sport shortly after Roach retired, when Interim Athletic Director Dan Viola—who died in 2010—was running the Department. When asked if the trustees should have waited until a permanent AD was in place to make such a major decision, Viola said, "To be honest with you, yeah, I probably think so. But I know a number of the trustees had been looking at the program for a number of years. I kind of felt, when Roach retired, that was their opportunity to act on it."

Viola came up with an alternative plan that would have spared baseball by reducing the scholarships and travel budgets for the men's and women's swimming and diving and track and field teams.

"I thought it was (a viable option)," Viola said. "But the trustees had already made up their mind, which I thought was a real shame."

In a letter to the *Laramie Boomerang*, printed in the January 31, 1996, edition, Roark wrote (4):

> *While the alternative to allocate spending on a tiered basis has some merit, we still would be reducing funding for other athletic programs to maintain baseball. I believe it is better to eliminate one program now so we can maintain or enhance strength in those remaining. . . .*
>
> *Dropping baseball will result in a savings of $200,000 a year. Half of that will be retained by the department to help support other athletic programs. Consequently, athletics will be contributing only $200,000 over two years to help make up for the budget shortfall. . . .*

I regret deeply having to discontinue baseball. I regret even more having to eliminate 45.5 faculty and staff positions, having to discontinue or curtail academic programs, having to reduce classroom and laboratory support budgets, and having to put off critical physical plant maintenance.

Lee Moon was hired as Wyoming's new Athletic Director after a national search. He had no real interest in bringing baseball back unless a donor wanted to step up and pay for the costs of the program.

"You'd love to have baseball, but they made the right decision," Moon said. ". . . what are you going to do? Roach made a recommendation that they drop track and field. There were some trustees and very high-powered alumni that had some interest in track and field.

"As I've come to know over seven years, that's the politics of Wyoming." (1)

Usually when the sore subject of Wyoming baseball is brought up in conversation, fans assume the program was axed due to Title IX. Clearly, it was more of a financial and political issue.

"January 20, 1996 was the day I was called in by Dan Viola. He told me that there was going to be no more baseball," said Dave Taylor, the UW Head Coach in 1995 and 1996. "His explanation was that it was a gender-equity issue, which was a flat out lie. If you drop baseball you could forever have track at the university. Dave Bonner had some vested interest in the track program and he's the one that kind of spearheaded the campaign to get of baseball instead. . . ."

"I understand why you would cut that sport based on the weather and the travel and all the class time kids are missing. But the way they went about it left a poor taste in everybody's mouth."

Taylor was a young, talented coach who could still relate to the Cowboys and what they were going through entering the 1996 season. Led by All-Conference selections Ron Cincera (shortstop), Rob Coddington (catcher) and Jeremy Schied (outfield), the proud 'Pokes went out in style with a 36-20 overall record and a third-place finish in the WAC behind longtime rivals BYU and New Mexico.

"I tried to sell them on the fact that they needed to have a good year for another Division I school to want to pick them up. That was motivating for them," Taylor said. "And to be the last team at a school with a rich baseball history . . . we wanted to make our mark before we saddled up and left town."

Wyoming remained in contention for a WAC title throughout the 1996 season until getting swept by BYU—10-6, 16-7 and 30-13—in an emotional three-game series May 3 and 4 at Cowboy Field. It was not just the end of days for Cowboys baseball, but the end of great rivalries against longtime foes such as the Cougars, Utes, Lobos and Rams.

"I'll never forget (BYU's) LeRoy Brown hitting a home run and sliding into home, and then he did a little break dance on the plate," Taylor recalled of the frustrating final home stand. "I couldn't stop myself from trying to get out there. I had to be restrained in dugout."

"I never really liked the way they went about their business. And every time we went over there we didn't get the calls. I never really felt BYU and Utah respected our program the way they should have."

Former Cowboys Head Coach, Bill Kinneberg, whose favorite stop in a lengthy baseball career was in Laramie, has built Utah into one of the best programs west of the Mississippi.

"Paul Roach is one of my heroes. He's one of the greatest people I've ever met," Kinneberg said. "He was the football coach and the Athletic Director, but he really cared about baseball, and he wanted it to succeed. I know every year he fought like heck to keep that program intact. And as soon as he announced his retirement, they dropped baseball."

Jim Gattis, UW's Head Coach in 1994-95, has met with a group about investing money to build an indoor baseball stadium in Laramie, with the idea of bringing baseball back to UW. He even has called the Athletic Department about the idea, which he admits is a "pipe dream."

A privately funded indoor stadium would certainly eliminate the weather issue and would allow the Cowboys to play a balanced schedule instead of spending the majority of the season on the road.

"Wyoming could be the Mecca for college baseball in that part of the country," Gattis said. "It could be the place where everybody wants to go to play baseball. What's not to like? Wyoming is a great place with great people."

More likely, Wyoming baseball will remain nothing but a memory. The immortal 1956 Cowboys will be the only team to ever represent the state and its university at the CWS.

"It hurt when they gave up baseball. It really did," said Ralph Vaughan, the ace of the 1956 staff. "We're awful proud to be the only team to go to the CWS. It's too bad it will never be done again."

Forty years after Wyoming's trip to Omaha, longtime Cowboy Head Coach, Bud Daniel, was inducted into the UW Athletics Hall of Fame. Daniel said Moon, who was hired in 1996 just after the decision was made to cut the baseball program, nearly spoiled the celebration.

"Moon really upset me at the party after my induction," Daniel said. "He said, 'I'm really upset about losing baseball, but if you can give me a check for a million dollars we can reinstate it.'"

"Several members of the 1956 team decided to cancel their financial support of the Athletic Department when baseball was cut."

Vaughan, who lives in Virginia, has driven to Charlottesville, VA and Knoxville, TN in recent years to support the UW football team.

Herb Manig moved to Laramie recently after retiring. He has season tickets for football, men's basketball and women's basketball.

"I donate to the Cowboy Joe club, but the biggest disappointment to me was the irony of 1996 being the year when the University canceled the program and also inducted Bud in the Hall of Fame," Manig said. "Talk about bittersweet."

So the official reason Wyoming cut baseball was to save $200,000 a year, but what the University's decision robbed the state of is priceless.

The majority of young men who came to Wyoming for baseball graduated. Many of them met their future wives in Laramie and have sent sons, daughters and grandchildren to the school they love, but would never had attended if not for the baseball program.

Over the years, the opportunity to play for the Cowboys changed countless lives for the better.

"I wasn't a great student, but I didn't want to go back to Chicago," said Jim Hoppe, one of the great players on the 'Pokes only CWS team, who Daniel recruited to Wyoming out of the Windy City during the 1950s. "I probably would have worked at a grocery store. Stepping off the train in Laramie to play baseball and get an education changed my life."

Hoppe moved to Casper after graduation and is now a retired educator. The only thing missing from his life in Wyoming is the beloved baseball program.

"They've sure lost a lot of good kids," Hoppe said.

The son of former UW and Major League great, Greg Brock—like many talented Colorado high school players

(Colorado and Colorado State also have dropped base-ball)—had to leave the area to pursue his college baseball dreams at Saint Louis University.

"Colorado has good baseball talent and trying to get these kids placed in out-of-state programs can be tough," said Brock, who built a prep powerhouse as a coach at Mountain View High School in Loveland, CO. "I think it's a disgrace for the kids in Colorado that there are not baseball programs at CU, CSU or Wyoming. There are 125 kids in this area who should be playing college baseball here and don't."

Imagine if Brock didn't get that scholarship offer from the Cowboys (the only program that recruited the future Los Angeles Dodgers standout), or if Art Howe didn't get a chance to play for Daniel, or if Jeff Huson didn't hone his skills at Cowboy Field?

There are a lot of talented young men out there missing out on those opportunities because of the demise of the treasure that was Wyoming baseball.

"I think anyone who's gone to Wyoming knows how special of a place it is," said Huson, whose wife is from Cheyenne and whose son used to wear a Casey Bramlet jersey to school. "People used to ask me all the time, when I was in the Majors, where I went to school. I'd say, 'Wyoming.' They'd say, 'They have a baseball program?' I'd say, 'They used to.'"

"I'm very proud to have gone to Wyoming."

There is no joy at Cowboy Field—the mighty 'Pokes have struck out.

Yankee Hall of Famer Lefty Gomez shows the famous "pinstripes" to Connie Daniel.

Cartoon of Bud Daniel to promote the semi-pro Basin League in Nebraska, North Dakota, and South Dakota.

Sources

Interviews with Greg Brock, Glenn "Bud" Daniel, Bill Ewing, Jim Gattis, Frank Goodie, Fritz Heiss, Jim Hoppe, Pat House, Art Howe, Jeff Huson, Bill Kinneberg, Herb Manig, Mike Mulvaney, Alan Simpson, Sky Smeltzer, Bob Sullivan, David Taylor and Ralph Vaughan were conducted during the winter and spring 2009-10. Player vignettes were written by the many great Cowboys themselves at the request of Daniel.

(1) *Casper Star-Tribune*, "Gone: Track and field won out over baseball when time came to cut a program," by Jack Daly, May 2, 2004.

(2) *Los Angeles Times*, "Jim Gattis Took Intensity to a Different Level," by Steve Elling, July 30, 1994.

(3) University of Wyoming, *Cowboys Baseball Media Guide*, February 1996.

(4) *Laramie Boomerang*, "UW baseball," January 31, 1996.

Books by Pearn and Associates, Inc.

Lost Cowboys: The Bud Daniel Story, and Wyoming Baseball,
    Ryan Thorburn

Black 14: The Rise, Fall and Rebirth of Wyoming Football,
    Ryan Thorburn

The Bone Hunters, Thom Hatch

The Dreamer and the Dream, Rick E. Roberts

Mathematics in Color, Joseph J. Kozma

Walking in Snow, John Knoepfle

I Look Around for my Life, John Knoepfle

A Lenten Journey Toward Christian Maturity, William E. Breslin

Ikaria: A Love Odyssey on a Greek Island, Anita Sullivan

The U Book, Photo Travel Journal in India, Nathan Pierce

Another Chance, Joe Naiman,

Goulash and Picking Pickles, Louise Hoffmann

Point Guard, Victor Pearn

Breinigsville, PA USA
06 October 2010
246797BV00006B/120/P